ALL I WANT.....

IS FOR YOU TO HEAR WHAT I HEAR

J WINES

WESTBOW
PRESS®
A DIVISION OF THOMAS NELSON
& ZONDERVAN

WestBow Press books may be ordered through booksellers or by contacting:

WestBow Press
A Division of Thomas Nelson & Zondervan
1663 Liberty Drive
Bloomington, IN 47403
www.westbowpress.com
1 (866) 928-1240

ISBN: 978-1-5127-4511-5 (sc)
ISBN: 978-1-5127-4513-9 (hc)
ISBN: 978-1-5127-4512-2 (e)

Library of Congress Control Number: 2016909015

Print information available on the last page.

WestBow Press rev. date: 6/10/2016

Contents

Dedicated to those who have ears to hear.

Matthew 13: 9–17

My heart is heavy,
Crushed because my eyes are open.
The visions too much to bear,
My eyes cry tears of blood.
Sitting, weeping in despair,
Gasping, hoping, and wishing.
Too much sorrow, too much pain.
Hands to reach, and hope to share.
What's the cure?
If I told you,
Would you believe me or even care?
The weight of your answer
Lies heavy on my heart.

Crimson tears flow down my face.

Preface

I see people hurting all around me. I see it in my own family, I see it in my community, and I see it on TV. It is all around the world. It breaks my heart!

I wish I could help everyone who hurts, who is searching for relief and for what life is meant to be. The problem is, I'm just a maintenance man at a small apartment complex in the suburbs of St. Louis. Who am I that I should talk and be heard? You see, for some reason the few I talk to, and even my own family, don't hear what I'm saying.

I can't hear what's being said in the programs on TV without turning it up so loud that everyone else complains that it's too loud. It makes no sense to me why when two people in a scene are speaking softly and quietly that movie producers feel the need to play background music that drowns out the words being said. Life is like that. It is so full of background noise that the noise drowns out what needs to be heard. I was fortunate to have heard the quiet message of hope, grace, contentment, and happiness through all the noise in the world. You see, my hearing defect causes background noise to dominate over what is being said, and the world has a hearing defect that causes the background noise of life to dominate over the quiet message of what life was created to be.

It is my desire and prayer that you might be able to hear what I heard. It is my hope that your ears might be opened that you might hear what I have to share. These words were never mine but were shared with me, and now I wish to share with you. There is hope because there is grace.

Acknowledgements

A young woman in our Bible study class shared that when she would ask her oldest son a question he would respond, "Do you want the Sunday school answer or the truth?"

To give recognition and appreciation for this work, which became a book, I must acknowledge that it became so only through the work of God's Holy Spirit. It was the Holy Spirit that inspired many different men to record God's word in the Bible. It was the Holy Spirit that taught and inspired many men down through the ages of time to write and share the wisdom given them by God. I am indebted to many of those men that God used to help me understand through their books, the life and relationship He created me to have.

I am a maintenance supervisor at a small apartment community in St. Louis, MO. I do not possess the ability to write a book, nor did I ever dream to do so. Yet here it is. Who do I acknowledge for this work? My answer is both the Sunday school answer and the truth. There is no way I could have done this. I am deeply humbled to have shared in this work with God.

Ad Majorem Dei Gloriam

Chapter 1

The Wounded Warrior

Are you tired of fighting and sore from your wounds? Are you tired of being knocked down every time you try to get up? Does it take all your strength just to draw your next breath? Are you confused as to whether your life has purpose or not? Do you sit in darkness and wonder why you were even born? Do you feel like no one sees you or hears you? Most of all, do you wonder where God is? Why does He not answer your cries for help? Does He not care?

Listen to what happened to Job, a man who loved God and worshipped Him with all his heart. A man whom God was well pleased in. A man whom God had blessed greatly with a large family and great wealth.

> Job was a man who lived in Uz. He was honest inside and out, a man of his word, who was totally devoted to God and hated evil with a passion. He had seven sons and three daughters. He was also very wealthy—seven thousand head of sheep, three thousand camels, five hundred teams of oxen, five hundred donkeys, and a huge staff of servants—the most influential man in all the East! (Job 1:1–3 MSG)

> Sometime later, while Job's children were having one of their parties at the home of the oldest son, a messenger came to Job and said, "The oxen were plowing and the donkeys grazing in the field next to us when Sabeans

attacked. They stole the animals and killed the field hands. I'm the only one to get out alive and tell you what happened." While he was still talking, another messenger arrived and said, "Bolts of lightning struck the sheep and the shepherds and fried them—burned them to a crisp. I'm the only one to get out alive and tell you what happened." While he was still talking, another messenger arrived and said, "Chaldeans coming from three directions raided the camels and massacred the camel drivers. I'm the only one to get out alive and tell you what happened." While he was still talking, another messenger arrived and said, "Your children were having a party at the home of the oldest brother when a tornado swept in off the desert and struck the house. It collapsed on the young people and they died. I'm the only one to get out alive and tell you what happened." Job got to his feet, ripped his robe, shaved his head, then fell to the ground and worshiped: Naked I came from my mother's womb, naked I'll return to the womb of the earth. God gives, God takes. God's name be ever blessed. Not once through all this did Job sin; not once did he blame God (Job 1:13–22 MSG).

Satan left God and struck Job with terrible sores. Job was ulcers and scabs from head to foot. They itched and oozed so badly that he took a piece of broken pottery to scrape himself, then went and sat on a trash heap, among the ashes. His wife said, "Still holding on to your precious integrity, are you? Curse God and be done with it!" He told her, "You're talking like an empty-headed fool. We take the good days from God —why not also the bad days?" Not once through all this did Job sin. He said nothing against God (Job 2:7–10 MSG).

Save me, God! The water is up to my throat and about to consume me! I have sunk in quicksand, and there is no stronghold for my feet. I have fallen into deep waters, and the flood is about to wash over me. I am exhausted and drained. My throat is dry and swollen; my voice fails me from calling to you. My eyes are bloodshot and burn from crying and searching the heavens for you. Where are you, God? I fear I am going down for the last time! (my paraphrase of Psalm 69:1–3)

Do you believe that if you are a good person life will treat you fairly? Do you believe that if you do everything God asks of you, you will not suffer? Do you think that God would allow innocent people to suffer? Do you think God is fair?

These are all questions that Job and his friends discussed. His friends thought that they were wise and knew what God was like. They thought that God thought like they did, and they spoke for God without His permission.

This is what God had to say about the way we think and the way God thinks:

> For my thoughts are not your thoughts, neither are your ways my ways, declares the LORD. For as the heavens are higher than the earth, so are my ways higher than your ways and my thoughts than your thoughts (Isaiah 55:8–9 ESV).

God tires of Job and his friends with their questioning of His fairness and judgments along with their self-righteousness and lack of wisdom.

I wish I could quote the whole response of God to Job and his friends, but that would be silly, so I encourage you to find the time to read the book of Job. Here is part of God's response:

> The Lord spoke to Job out of a storm. He said, "Who do you think you are to disagree with my plans? You do not know what you are talking about. Get ready to stand up for yourself. I will ask you some questions. Then I want you to answer me. Where were you when I laid the earth's foundation? Tell me, if you know. Who measured it? I am sure you know! Who stretched a measuring line across it? What was it built on? Who laid its most important stone? (Job 38:1–6 NIrV)

The Lord continued, "I am the Mighty One. Will the man who argues with me correct me? Let him who brings charges against me answer me!" Then the Lord spoke to Job out of the storm. He said, "Get ready to stand up for yourself. I will ask you some more questions. Then I want you to answer me. Would you dare to claim that I am not being fair? Would you judge me in order to make yourself seem right? Is your arm as powerful as mine is? Can your voice thunder as mine does? Then put on glory and beauty as if they were your clothes. Also put honor and majesty on. Let loose your great anger. Look at those who are proud and bring them low. Look at proud people and bring them down. Crush those who are evil right where they are. Bury their bodies in the dust together. Cover their faces in the grave. Then I myself will admit to you that your own right hand can save you" (Job 40:1–2, 6–14 NIrV).

Doug Herman was a modern-day Job. Here is his story:

Doug and Evon Herman had answered God's call, and Doug was studying and preparing for full-time ministry. On February 19, 1985, they had their first child, Joshua. During the delivery, Evon was given two units of blood. Eighteen months later they were told one of the units of blood had been found to be HIV-positive and that Evon had tested positive for HIV as well. The doctors informed them that the HIV virus would probably cause AIDS, which had no cure. Doug and Joshua were not infected with the virus. Doug and Evon could not understand how this could have happened. They were good Christians, they were in God's ministry, they were not drug users, and they were faithful in their marriage. They had dedicated their lives to God's ministry. God was supposed to be their protection.

On November 4, 1988, Ashli Nicole was born. She grew, was crawling, and seemed to be as normal as any other baby. The Hermans believed God had rewarded their faith and saved Ashli from the virus. When Ashli was nine months old, the virus set in; Ashli could no longer sit or hold her head up.

In a two-month period, Doug's life and faith came crashing down. Tests revealed Ashli was an AIDS baby at the age of six months. In this same time frame his grandfather, who was a loving Christian man, died of liver cancer. Doug also learned that his youngest brother had AML (acute myeloblastic leukemia). If things weren't bad enough, two months before Ashli died, Doug's church board decided that they no longer wished to keep Doug on staff and would not renew his position with the church. Doug was now without a means of income and insurance.

At eleven months old, all Ashli could do was wiggle her feet and hands, scream, and cry. Early in January 1991, Ashli, a little older than two years old, reached the point where the doctors called Doug in for a conference. Doug was given the choice to go two more days with aggressive medication and death or to shut off the life support machine and Ashli would probably die in two hours. After friends and family said their good-byes to Ashli, Doug went in to say his final good-bye. The nurse shut off the machine, and Ashli took two breaths and died. Evon was too sick to be with her daughter as she passed on to be with the Lord.

Eight months later Doug was called again into the conference room with the doctors. Doug was given the same choices, only this time they were for Evon: two days of suffering and death or two hours of suffering and death. Doug told the doctors, "Let my wife go home; I don't want her to suffer any longer." Evon died on September 9, 1991. Eight months later Doug's brother passed away.

Doug, like Job, could not understand why God would allow these things to happen. He was serving God. God was supposed to protect him and his family. None of this made any sense at all. Doug was angry and hurt at God. He wanted a face-to-face talk with God like Job had had. Doug, like Job, was basically telling God he was not fair; he was not just. Doug was doing what God asked him to do. He had answered his call to serve. He was being faithful. He was ministering to God's people. How could this happen to a family that loved God and that God loved greatly? Where was the justice? [1]

What are your expectations about life?

Let's be honest—sometimes life sucks! Life can suck the life out of you if you let it. If you are alive, you will suffer pain. Hopefully we are spared the extremes that Job and Doug Herman went through. Nonetheless, know this truth: life is difficult, harsh, and painful. Difficulties will happen to everyone. They will happen to you if they haven't already. It makes no difference how good you are or how bad you are.

When we can accept the fact that life has suffering and we are not immune to it, then we can move through it without needing to know "Why me?"

Difficulty and suffering have been part of life since Adam and Eve were expelled from the garden. Abel, with whom God was well pleased, was murdered by his brother, Cain. Joseph's brothers planned to kill him but sold him into slavery instead. Joseph, being a godly man, was also falsely accused of rape because he refused to sleep with his master's wife, and he was sent to prison. David spent many years running for his life from King Saul.

Obviously, suffering happens to the good and to the bad. Jesus stated in Matthew 5:45, "He causes the sun to shine on the evil and the good, and sends rain on the just and the unjust."

Our God is not a distant god. Our God is not a god lacking in human experience, one lacking knowledge of emotional and physical pain and suffering. As our God entered our world through his Son Jesus Christ in human form—living, eating, breathing, and drinking as the rest of us— He suffered much pain and anguish.

In Isaiah 53, we are told that He came with no form or majesty that we should look up to Him, no beauty that we should desire Him. He was despised and rejected, a man of sorrows and acquainted with grief. He had done no violence, and there was no deceit in His mouth.

He was hated, mocked, and made fun of. He was hunted like a criminal. He was betrayed by one of His own friends. He was spit upon and slapped, and false accusations were made against Him. Talk about mental and emotional stress. Listen to what Luke had to say about Jesus as he prayed in the garden just before his arrest and the things that were to take place:

> And being in an agony he prayed more earnestly; and his sweat became like great drops of blood falling down to the ground (Luke 22:44 ESV).

Have you ever agonized over anything that caused you to sweat, much less sweat drops of blood?

Who could forget Mel Gibson's depiction of Jesus's final hours in The Passion? The piercing of the crown of thorns into His head as the blood ran down. The whipping of the cat-o-nine tails as the bloody skin is ripped from his back almost to the point of death? The weight of the cross as He is made to carry it till He falls from exhaustion? The pounding of the hammer as it drives the spikes through His hands and feet, or the thud as the cross is dropped into the hole to hold the cross upright? The pain of pushing up on His nailed feet just to take another breath?

And if that wasn't enough, the feeling of being deserted by your father? Asking; where are you God? Why don't you answer me?

Listen to His cry from the cross:

> My God, my God, why have you forsaken me? Why are you so far from saving me, from the words of my groaning? O my God, I cry by day, but you do not answer, and by night, but I find no rest (Psalm 22:1–2 ESV).

I dare not say that our suffering compares to Christ's, but is this not the same cry that comes from the depths of our hurt and depression?

Here is some insight to God's wisdom in Isaiah about His Son's purpose.

> Still, it's what GOD had in mind all along, to crush him with pain. The plan was that he give himself as an offering for sin so that he'd see life come from it—life, life, and more life. And GOD's plan will deeply prosper through him" (Isaiah 53:10 MSG).

In our suffering we have become as a wounded warrior lying in wait, our wound open, not knowing if healing will come. If we are wounded in battle, we don't ask why. It's a known truth of war. If we go through suffering in life, we should not ask why; it's a known truth of life. Then the question should not be why, but who? Who will heal me and bring me back to my feet? Who is the Great Healer? Who is in control? The answer is God.

Back to Doug Herman ...

During the time when Ashli was nineteen months old, Doug took Joshua to get an inoculation before his son started kindergarten.

> When they stuck him with the needle, Josh looked straight at me. Looking deep into my eyes as I firmly held his head he cried "Daddy!" It was only one word, but his look said a million words. "Daddy, why the pain? Ouch, Daddy! Why are you letting them hurt me? I thought you were my father! It's not my fault. Why, Daddy? I thought you loved me."

> Josh's face reflected pain. It showed fear. But he also had a startling look of disappointment—like I had let him down.

> My eyes burned with tears as my mind suddenly raced to the familiar phrases I had uttered months before. "Why, God? I thought You loved me! I thought You were my Father! Why, Daddy? Why?"

Doug said that God spoke to him in that moment and simply told him, "It's the same with you and Me."

> A new understanding of who He is flooded my heart. You see, if I could explain the full reason for the inoculation to my son, I would. I love him. I would die for him. But even if I explained it, he wouldn't grasp it. For he can only understand simple, concrete thought. Until his mind matures, he can't understand abstract thoughts such as eternity ... inertia ... inoculation!

> So it is with our heavenly Father. While we can handle some complex thoughts, God is divine. He is all-knowing! His level of thought so exceeds our own that we can

never fully understand the reasons why He acts as He does. Yet if He could explain all the answers to our whys, He would. Right now, the answers would go right over our heads and we would label them "illogical." Many circumstances in life don't make sense. But that does not mean He does not love us. He does. So much so that He would die for us ... and did. [2]

If God is going to use you, He will allow you to pass through many trials, hardships, and sufferings that were not really meant for you. They were meant by God to shape you and mold you so that you might understand and be compassionate to what comes to pass in the lives of others around you and never be surprised.

God's road is the way of suffering, for some greater than others, but nonetheless suffering is the way He has chosen to bring glory to Himself. When we travel down that road of suffering, we don't realize what God is doing and we tend to misunderstand. It is only in our relationship to Jesus Christ that we can begin to understand what God is working to accomplish through our suffering. [3]

Through the pain we suffer we are able to offer hope to those who are hopeless. We have walked through what God has laid before us so that we may save the lives of others who are in despair ... so that we may bring them before God.

When we share the experience of our healing with fellow warriors, it brings purpose to our wounds. Because of our wounds, we are able to share in the healing of the lives of fellow warriors, being instruments of hope and encouragement. We can be the mentor who offers genuine compassionate guidance that coaches them back to a healthier life. Offer what God has offered to you—compassion and patience.

Chapter 2

The Battle with God

What makes us wounded warriors? Is it not because we have been wounded in the battle for life? What is our battle and with whom? If you do not know God, then your first and foremost battle is with God! There are no conscientious objectors in the battle with God. You cannot refuse to fight the battle against God on any grounds.

Are we at war with God? That depends.

Every human being will fight the battle of salvation with God:

> So then every one of us shall give account of himself to
> God (Romans 14:12 KJV).

That battle with God will bring you to a point where you will either surrender and except His terms through Jesus Christ, which bring everlasting life, or you will refuse to surrender and continue to rebel against Him, which brings everlasting death—not death in the terms that we understand death, but death in terms of existing in a lake of fire that was created for satan and his followers, where you will be tormented day and night forever and ever (Revelation 20:10–15, Matthew 25:41).

First, you have to admit that there is a battle, that you are at odds with God. You are a rebel. Whether aggressively or passively, you still rebel against God's law.

> It is written, "No one is right with God, no one at all. No
> one understands. No one trusts in God. All of them have

turned away. They have all become worthless. No one does anything good, no one at all." (Psalms 14:1–3; 53:1–3; Ecclesiastes 7:20) "Their throats are like open graves. With their tongues they tell lies." (Psalm 5:9) "The words from their lips are like the poison of a snake." (Psalm 140:3) "Their mouths are full of curses and bitterness." (Psalm 10:7) "They run quickly to commit murder. They leave a trail of failure and pain. They do not know the way of peace." (Isaiah 59:7,8) "They don't have any respect for God." (Psalm 36:1) (Romans 3:10–18 NIrV).

So what will we bring to the battlefield? We have already lost before we began. We were condemned at birth, even before birth at the garden with Adam and Eve:

And the LORD God commanded the man, saying, "You may surely eat of every tree of the garden, but of the tree of the knowledge of good and evil you shall not eat, for in the day that you eat of it you shall surely die" (Genesis 2:16–17 ESV).

So why didn't Adam and Eve die right then?

The Lord is not slow to keep his promise. He is not slow in the way some people understand it. He is patient with you. He doesn't want anyone to be destroyed. Instead, he wants all people to turn away from their sins (2 Peter 3:9 NIrV).

God speaks the truth. God warns us that there are consequences for our rebellion and sin. The judgment is death, but God wants no one to perish. God withholds executing the sentence, giving time that all may change their ways, turn to God, and accept the gift and payment made through His Son Jesus Christ.

Many times in the Bible, God's Word will have a double meaning. When God told Adam that he would surely die when he ate of the tree of knowledge of good and evil, He was not just speaking of the physical death. Because man was created in the image of God, and God had breathed His spirit into man, there would be a spiritual death as well. There will be a judgment of the spirit life, and an eternal death sentence will be passed as well on that life:

> Then I saw a great white throne and him who was seated on it. From his presence earth and sky fled away, and no place was found for them. And I saw the dead, great and small, standing before the throne, and books were opened. Then another book was opened, which is the book of life. And the dead were judged by what was written in the books, according to what they had done. And the sea gave up the dead who were in it, Death and Hades gave up the dead who were in them, and they were judged, each one of them according to what they had done. Then Death and Hades were thrown into the lake of fire. This is the second death, the lake of fire. And if anyone's name was not found written in the book of life, he was thrown into the lake of fire (Revelation 20:11–15 EVS).

Because of Adam and Eve's rebellion against God's command not to eat of the tree of knowledge of good and evil, the death sentence was passed down to all of humanity. The original sin was rebellion, but all sin has its consequences, and the knowledge of good and evil was passed down from generation to generation. So now we decide, as did Adam and Eve, whether to passively or aggressively, by omission or commission, determine what is good or evil for ourselves ... ignoring all the time that God is the one that sets the standards and laws of good and evil. We rebel against God by choosing the enticement of evil and neglecting to do what is right and good.

You say you're a good person, that you have done good all your life—at least good enough:

> The LORD saw that the wickedness of man was great in the earth, and that every intention of the thoughts of his heart was only evil continually (Genesis 6:5 ESV).

[F]or all have sinned and fall short of the glory of God (Romans 3:23 ESV).

"For from within, out of the heart of man, come evil thoughts, sexual immorality, theft, murder, adultery, coveting, wickedness, deceit, sensuality, envy, slander, pride, foolishness. All these evil things come from within, and they defile a person" (Mark 7:21–23, ESV).

For as he thinketh in his heart, so is he (Proverbs 23:7 KJV).

"But I say to you that everyone who looks at a woman with lustful intent has already committed adultery with her in his heart" (Matthew 5:28 ESV).

We are hopelessly lost to ourselves. Even our thoughts are sin lurking at the door like a cancer waiting to consume us.

Jesus tells an interesting story relating to the kingdom of heaven in Matthew 18:23–27.

Jesus says the kingdom of heaven is compared to a king calling in the debts that are owed to him. He calls in one particular servant who owes him ten thousand talents. No way can the servant even begin to pay this enormous debt, and the king orders him and his whole family to be thrown in prison till the debt is paid in full. The servant falls to the ground and begs the king to give him time, that he will pay it back. The king has compassion for the servant and forgives the whole debt.

Now this story goes on to show that this servant no sooner leaves the king who so graciously had forgiven him his debt, and he now hunts down one of his debtors, a fellow servant, and demands payment from him. This man's debt was minor compared to his own, which had just been forgiven. When his debtor begs for mercy and time to pay, he shows no mercy and has him thrown in prison till the debt is paid in full.

When the king hears how the debtor threatened his fellow servant and imprisoned him, the king throws the debtor he had just forgiven in prison till his complete debt be paid to the king.

The story was to show that we have been forgiven of much by God and so we are to forgive others. If we don't, then God will not forgive us.

What is interesting about this story is the differences between the amounts owed. The amount owed by the servant to the king was ten thousand talents, and the debtor to the servant owed one hundred denarii.

According to the footnotes in the Life Application Study Bible, one talent was worth more than fifteen years' wages of a laborer, and the denarius was a day's wages. [4]

Let's put this into perspective. At this time the minimum wage in Missouri is $7.50. With the standard day being eight hours of work, then a day's wages for a laborer would be $60.00, making 100 denarii equivalent to $6,000.00, the amount owed to the debtor to the king by his fellow servant.

Now, based on a 40-hour workweek, there are 2,080 hours in one year, so a day's wage of $60.00 times 2,080 hours equals $15,600.00 a year. Using the equation above that one talent equals at least 15 years' wages, we find that one talent equals $234,000.00. Ten thousand times $234,000.00 equals $2,340,000,000.00. If that doesn't boggle your mind, try it this way: one talent equals 15 years of labor to pay back the debt. Multiply that by 10,000, since he owed 10,000 talents, so he would have to work for 150,000 years to pay back the debt he owed the king!

I am doomed. What can I possibly do to save myself? I am not a bad person, but God's expectations are too high for me. God wants obedience, and I am mixed with rebellion. God wants joy, and I am mixed with bitterness. God wants giving, and I am mixed with selfishness. God wants peace, and I am mixed with resentment. God wants love, and I am mixed with anger. I am hopelessly unable to remove the evil that resides in me.

> What the law says, it says to those who are ruled by the law. Its purpose is to shut every mouth and make the whole world accountable to God. So it can't be said that anyone will be made right with God by obeying the law. Not at all! The law makes us more aware of our sin (Romans 3: 19–20 NIrV).

I cry out like Isaiah, Woe is me; how terrible! I melt in great fear of the LORD! I am undone. I am a man that sins with my thoughts, my mouth, and my hands. I live in a land of people consumed in sin! The LORD GOD Almighty has been revealed to me. I fear for my life (my paraphrase of Isaiah 6:5).

Do you get it? Can you see it?

It is impossible to pay back the debt we owe the King, God.

> When the disciples heard this, they were very astonished and said, "Then who can be saved?" And looking at them Jesus said to them, "With people this is impossible, but with God all things are possible" (Matthew 19: 25–26 NASB).

Imagine a man standing at the gates of heaven. Peter tells the man he needs one thousand points to get in. Peter asks him what has he done to earn his points.

The man was a bit surprised and said, "I've never heard that before. Well, let me see … I was raised in a Christian family and have always been a church member. I have Sunday school attendance pins that go down to the floor. I went to a Christian college and graduate school and have led hundreds of people to Christ. Before I died, I was an elder in my church and supportive of the people of God. I have three children—two boys and a girl. My oldest boy is a pastor, and the younger has a ministry to the poor. My daughter and her husband are missionaries. I have always tithed, giving as much as 30 percent of my income to God's work at the end. In my job as a bank executive, I worked with the poor in our city who were trying to get low-income mortgages."

"How am I doing so far?" he asked Peter.

"That's one point," Peter said. "What else have you done?"

"Good Lord … have mercy!" the man said in frustration.

"That's it!" Peter said. "Welcome home." [5]

When you think about the high standards God has set, that Jesus said that if you have hate in your heart, it is the same as murder. If you look at a woman with lust, it is the same as adultery. It becomes clear that the Ten Commandments were not to show the way into heaven, but to show how utterly helpless we are, that our only hope is to fall before God and cry for mercy!

There is NOTHING that we can do but cry to our Creator, our God, our Father for mercy and forgiveness.

Secondly, we must believe that Jesus came to pay the debt for our rebellion against God and our wrongdoing.

Jesus has paid the debt for us; the King, God, has forgiven our debt because Jesus his only Son has paid it for us. Jesus came to this earth in human form only to pay that debt, nailed to the cross, with his body. He called out, "It is finished," and gave up his spirit (John 19:30). It was over and our debt was paid in full; all was accomplished that God had sent him to do. It was set from the beginning that his death was the purpose for Christ being born a man. It took the perfect submission of the sinless Christ man to make right the debt owed due to our sin and rebellion, from the first man who started it, Adam, to the last man who finished it, Jesus the Christ, the only Son of God.

> For the wages of sin is death, but the *free gift* of God is eternal life in Christ Jesus our Lord (Romans 6:23 ESV; emphasis is mine).

> Whoever believes in him is not condemned, but whoever does not believe is condemned already, because he has not believed in the name of the only Son of God (John 3:18 ESV).

But because of God's great love, compassion, and grace, through the work of his Son, He offers acquittal to those who believe and except his gift.

> This is how much God loved the world: He gave his Son, his one and only Son. And this is why: so that no one need be destroyed; by believing in him, anyone can have a whole and lasting life. God didn't go to all the trouble of sending his son merely to point an accusing finger, telling the world how bad it was. He came to help, to put the world right again. Anyone who trusts in him is acquitted; anyone who refuses to trust him has long since

been under the death sentence without knowing it. And why? Because of that person's failure to believe in the one-of-a-kind Son of God when introduced to him (John 3:16–18 MSG).

God forewarned and commanded that rebellion would be punished with death. Payment of that punishment had to be made, and Jesus came to Earth in the form of a man to pay the debt for us. He was perfect and knew no sin, but He took on our sin and rebellion and suffered our punishment that we could be made right in God's eyes. He took on our death that we might live forever with Him.

At just the right time Christ died for ungodly people. He died for us when we had no power of our own. It is unusual for anyone to die for a godly person. Maybe someone would be willing to die for a good person. But here is how God has shown his love for us. While we were still sinners, Christ died for us. The blood of Christ has made us right with God. So we are even more sure that Jesus will save us from God's anger. Once we were God's enemies. But we have been brought back to him because his Son has died for us. Now that God has brought us back, we are even more secure. We know that we will be saved because Christ lives. (Romans 5:6–10 NIrV).

Finally, confess Jesus Christ as your Savior.

I call heaven and earth to witness against you today, that I have set before you life and death, blessing and curse. Therefore choose life, that you and your offspring may live, loving the LORD your God, obeying his voice and holding fast to him, for he is your life and length of days (Deuteronomy 30:19–20 ESV).

Conviction of sin is a rare and strange thing when it hits the hearts of people. Before it strikes, it makes no sense to us because we think we are good and moral. Jesus said when the Holy Spirit came, He would convict people of sin, and when He stirred up the conscience to the presence of God, it was no longer how we relate to other people, but our relationship with God. We realize, like David, that "against you God, and only You have I committed this great sin, before your eyes have I done this evil!" (Psalms 51:4) The conviction of sin, forgiveness, and holiness are so much as one that those who are forgiven become holy, and the fruit of that is when they are the opposite of what they used to be by the grace of God and through the power of the Holy Spirit. Conviction and repentance always bring people to this point—they have sinned before God!

The life of Christ in you through the Holy Spirit will make you conscious of your need for repentance, and never consciously mention your holiness. Christianity is all about turning from your sins and asking for forgiveness. Should you ever lose the value of repentance, search yourself to see if you have grown cold to the Holy Spirit. [6]

> If we say we have no sin, we deceive ourselves, and the truth is not in us. If we confess our sins, he is faithful and just to forgive us our sins and to cleanse us from all unrighteousness. If we say we have not sinned, we make him a liar, and his word is not in us (1 John 1:8–10 ESV).

Has the Holy Spirit convicted you of your sins? Quit worrying about what you've done right or wrong and how to fix yourself. But put all your strength and heart into your relationship with God, and all else will follow.

> "Give your entire attention to what God is doing right now, and don't get worked up about what may or may not happen tomorrow. God will help you deal with whatever hard things come up when the time comes (Matthew 6:34 MSG).

> Jesus replied," 'Love the Lord your God with all your heart and with all your soul. Love him with all your mind' (Deuteronomy 6:5) (Matthew 22:37 NIrV).

Our greatest concern in life is not so much consciously being obedient, but the perseverance of our relationship with God the Father through his only Son Jesus Christ, our brother. The most important thing is our relationship and friendship with Jesus.

There is another battle to be fought with God—the battle of will before God. His Spirit captures me and brings me before Him alone to fight the battle; it is between me and Him, no one else. If I do not fight this battle first in spirit with God, I will lose my battles in the external world. It is a strange battle indeed! If I stand firm in my will and say to God that reason and tangible proofs will be the deciding factors when I am confronted by matters of faith, then I lose the battle all the while thinking I won because I got my way. In reality I have lost the battle. I do not trust God at His word. How can I have confidence to win battles in the external world when I have lost the battle in the spiritual world before God? I have lost by winning. If I surrender my will to God and let His Word and promises be the power of my actions by faith, then I have won by losing. Get alone with God, and fight it out before Him. Get the battle settled once and for all. The duration of this battle depends on you, not God. He has as long as it takes. There is no power over the person who has won this battle by surrendering his or her will to God. [7]

Jacob's wrestling with God ...

> But Jacob stayed behind by himself, and a man wrestled with him until daybreak. When the man saw that he couldn't get the best of Jacob as they wrestled, he deliberately threw Jacob's hip out of joint. The man said, "Let me go; it's daybreak." Jacob said, "I'm not letting you go 'til you bless me." The man said, "What's your name?" He answered, "Jacob." The man said, "But no longer. Your name is no longer Jacob. From now on it's Israel (God-Wrestler); you've wrestled with God and you've come through." Jacob asked, "And what's your name?" The man said, "Why do you want to know my name?" And then, right then and there, he blessed him. Jacob named the place Peniel (God's Face) because, he said, "I saw God face-to-face and lived to tell the story!" (Genesis 32:24–28 MSG).

This is a very interesting story. Who can fight with God and win? God is all-powerful; God defeated satan and his angels. A human is no feat for Him, yet it sounds like God could not get the better of Jacob. Even after dislocating Jacob's hip, He asks Jacob to let Him go. Jacob refuses to let go of God and tells Him he will not let go until God blesses him. Oh, the audacity of Jacob! What in the world is really going on here? What is God showing us through this incident between God and Jacob?

It was not God's desire to defeat Jacob, for He could have crushed Jacob in a New York minute. God is so cool and so wise! God let Jacob battle with Him until He knew Jacob was ready to listen and accept what blessing God had for him. Do you see what God is telling you here? He's saying, Let's battle this out. You're depressed, you're angry, mad at me; you think I am unfair and uncaring. He's saying, Yell it as loud as you can; let your anger out at me. I am big enough to take it. And don't you dare quit on me; let us battle it out! And when I wound you, hold tight to Me and persevere. And when I see that you are ready to listen and accept my blessing, I will give it to you.

So have you surrendered? Have you accepted God's terms of peace? Isn't it amazing that in terms of the world, when we surrender we lose and give up possessions and freedom, but with God we gain many new gifts and a greater freedom. His greatest gift was the sacrifice of His only Son Jesus. Can you imagine having to admit defeat, surrendering to the king and expecting death as your punishment for your rebellion, but the king does just the opposite? He gives you gifts and makes you a joint heir with his only Son to His kingdom?

> [B]ut you have received the Spirit of adoption as sons, by whom we cry, "Abba! Father!" The Spirit himself bears witness with our spirit that we are children of God, and if children, then heirs—heirs of God and fellow heirs with Christ (Romans 8:15b–17a ESV).

Is that the story between God and you?

If someone gives you a gift, are you not going to check it out, see what it is and how to use it? If you're given a piece of land, would you not go check it out? If you were to receive a kingdom, would you not check it out and see all there was to it?

So if you are a joint heir of the kingdom of God with His Son Jesus, listen to what your new brother wants you to do first.

> "But seek first the kingdom of God and his righteousness, and all these things will be added to you" (Matthew 6:33 ESV).

So first and most importantly, *above all else in life*, Jesus wants us to search out the vastness of our Father's kingdom and His gracious righteousness. How do we do that?

First, if we belong to the kingdom by our acceptance of what Jesus has done for us, He will place a desire in our hearts to learn, to know, to experience all that we can grasp about our heavenly Father and His son—our King, our priest, our brother Jesus Christ.

By faith we must determine to fight through all obstacles to place God first in *all things* … to search His Word to learn who He is and what He expects of us … to determine to make our relationship with God above all others.

Through the power of the Holy Spirit we must discipline ourselves to be obedient to all that God's Word teaches us.

Chapter 3

The Need to Be Humble

What causes quarrels and what causes fights among you? Is it not this, that your passions are at war within you? You desire and do not have, so you murder. You covet and cannot obtain, so you fight and quarrel. You do not have, because you do not ask. You ask and do not receive, because you ask wrongly, to spend it on your passions. You adulterous people! Do you not know that friendship with the world is enmity with God? Therefore whoever wishes to be a friend of the world makes himself an enemy of God. Or do you suppose it is to no purpose that the Scripture says, "He yearns jealously over the spirit that he has made to dwell in us"? But he gives more grace. Therefore it says, "God opposes the proud, but gives grace to the humble." Submit yourselves therefore to God. Resist the devil, and he will flee from you. Draw near to God, and he will draw near to you. Cleanse your hands, you sinners, and purify your hearts, you double-minded. Be wretched and mourn and weep. Let your laughter be turned to mourning and your joy to gloom. Humble yourselves before the Lord, and he will exalt you (James 4:1–10 ESV).

> Likewise, you who are younger, be subject to the elders. Clothe yourselves, all of you, with humility toward one another, for "God opposes the proud but gives grace to the humble." Humble yourselves, therefore, under the mighty hand of God so that at the proper time he may exalt you, casting all your anxieties on him, because he cares for you. Be sober-minded; be watchful. Your adversary the

devil prowls around like a roaring lion, seeking someone to devour. Resist him, firm in your faith, knowing that the same kinds of suffering are being experienced by your brotherhood throughout the world. And after you have suffered a little while, the God of all grace, who has called you to his eternal glory in Christ, will himself restore, confirm, strengthen, and establish you. To him be the dominion forever and ever. Amen (1 Peter 5:5–11 ESV).

So how do we humble ourselves? Realize our origin? We are nothing ... we are filthy rags.

We have all become like one who is unclean, and all our righteous deeds are like a polluted garment. We all fade like a leaf, and our iniquities, like the wind, take us away. There is no one who calls upon your name, who rouses himself to take hold of you; for you have hidden your face from us, and have made us melt in the hand of our iniquities. But now, O LORD, you are our Father; we are the clay, and you are our potter; we are all the work of your hand (Isaiah 64:6–8 ESV).

From dust we came and to dust we shall return ...

"By the sweat of your face you shall eat bread, till you return to the ground, for out of it you were taken; for you are dust, and to dust you shall return" (Genesis 3:19 ESV).

We are liars ...

God is true, even though every human being is a liar. It is written, "You are right when you sentence me. You are fair when you judge me" (Psalm 51:4). (Romans 3:4b NIrV)

We must give up the charade of thinking we are anything, thinking that we are even deserving of God's care. God's Spirit will show us that we need to give up our claim to ourselves as well. Will I give up my rights to myself, my possessions, my affections, everything to be dead to self but alive in Christ? We are nothing in self but everything in Christ.

When we see ourselves in the light of God, it is not the horrible sins we commit in the flesh that bother us, but the audacity of pride in our hearts against Jesus Christ. When this light is shone in your heart, conviction will pierce you with shame and horror. [8]

Selfhood, that semiconscious realm of self, is the outer wall that wraps around the inner spiritual life. It alienates and isolates people. When we confuse selfhood with our spiritual life, we become isolated. God created selfhood as a protection for our spiritual life. You can see this as one of the main characteristics of a child. The child uses this realm of self to separate and categorize people as to trust or not to trust, to protect his inner being, his spirit. We must yield our selfhood, our little kingdom of self that we play king to, to God so that we might have fellowship with Him. Our selfhood counterfeits spirituality like lust counterfeits love. God created human nature for Himself; we have corrupted it with the realm of self for our own desires.

The main characteristics of our selfhood are self-will and independence. By insisting on our selfhood, we prevent spiritual growth more than any other way. When you say you can't believe, it's because your little kingdom of self blocks it; it doesn't fit in with what you have already decreed. The spirit, on the other hand, cannot help but to believe. Be attentive when God is working within you. God will bring you to the boundaries of your little kingdom of self, where a choice will have to be made. You will either choose not to surrender or to surrender, which brings down the walls of your little kingdom of self, letting the spiritual life become visible. The Holy Spirit reveals that every time it comes down to this one thing—it is your little kingdom of self that refuses to reconcile to your brother. God wants to bring you into a relationship with Himself, but you must be willing to give up your right to yourself: "If any man will come unto me, he must deny himself" (Matthew 16:24). Humble yourself; deny your independence, your right to self. Open the gates, tear down the walls of your selfhood, yield your little kingdom to God, and let the real life, the spirit life, grow. [9]

Chapter 4

The Holy Spirit

Listen to the Holy Spirit ...

Romans 6:16 tells us, "[W]e are slaves to the one we obey."

When I think about what it is that controls me, I must first come to the conclusion that I'm the one responsible for being controlled. I am a slave to myself because somewhere along the line I yielded to myself. I cannot blame anyone else; I made the choice myself. As well, if I obey God, it is because I yielded to God.

Should a child yield to selfishness, it will become a most restraining domination. There is no power in the human nature of one's self to break the enslavement of a disposition that one has surrendered to. Yield just once to anything in the realm of coveting and desire, though you may hate yourself for doing so, you will find that you are now enslaved to it. You will find there is no power in the human soul to break free. You must humble yourself and surrender to the power of the Lord Jesus Christ. He is the only one that can break the dominating power that you have yielded to.

You may say, "I can give up that habit anytime I like." You will find that you cannot; it completely controls you because you gave into it willingly. You can claim Scripture that says you can overcome and at the same time still live a life of slavery to yourself. Surrendering yourself and obeying Jesus will break every type of slavery. [10]

> Don't live under the control of your sinful nature. If you
> do, you will think about what your sinful nature wants.

Live under the control of the Holy Spirit. If you do, you will think about what the Spirit wants. The way a sinful person thinks leads to death. But the mind controlled by the Spirit brings life and peace. The sinful mind is at war with God. It does not obey God's law. It can't. Those who are controlled by their sinful nature can't please God. But your sinful nature does not control you. The Holy Spirit controls you. The Spirit of God *lives in you.* Anyone who does not have the Spirit of Christ does not belong to Christ (emphasis mine; Romans 8:5–9 NIrV).

"The Holy Spirit gives life. The body means nothing at all. The words I have spoken to you are from the Spirit. They give life" (John 6:63 NIrV).

In ourselves we are not able to claim anything for ourselves. The power to do what we do comes from God. He has given us the power to serve under a new covenant. The covenant is not based on the written Law of Moses. It comes from the Holy Spirit. The written Law kills, but the Spirit gives life (2 Corinthians 3:5–6 NIrV).

What or who is this Holy Spirit? What do I need to know about the Holy Spirit?

Paul asked some disciples in Ephesus if they had received the Holy Spirit. They answered no, we didn't even know there was such a Holy Spirit (Acts 19:2).

There is a danger in the lack of knowledge ...

Having a lack of knowledge is a dangerous thing. God told Isaiah that his people had gone into captivity because they lacked knowledge (Isaiah 5:13). In Hosea 4:6, God said, "My people are destroyed for lack of knowledge."

Many new and even old Christians are held captive and even destroyed by sin because they have no knowledge of the Holy Spirit. They do not know the Holy Spirit, His purpose, or His work in the mind and heart of the believer who accepts Christ's sacrifice on the cross for our sins.

You also became believers in Christ. That happened
when you heard the message of truth. It was the good
news about how you could be saved. *When you believed,*
he marked you with a seal. The seal is the Holy Spirit
that he promised (emphasis mine; Ephesians 1:13 NIrV).

Know this *very important truth:* when you were saved by accepting
Christ and all that he did for you on the cross, you were marked as a child
of God at that exact moment by the Holy Spirit, who came to live inside
you to be your helper in this new life you have received from Jesus Christ,
the only Son of God.

"And I will ask the Father, and he will give you another
Helper, to be with you forever, even the Spirit of truth,
whom the world cannot receive, because it neither sees
him nor knows him. You know him, for he dwells with
you and will be in you. (John 14;16-17 ESV)

"But the Helper, the Holy Spirit, whom the Father will
send in my name, he will teach you all things and bring
to your remembrance all that I have said to you" (John
14:26 ESV).

So we have learned that the Holy Spirit is received at the moment of
our salvation in Christ Jesus (Ephesians 1:13). The Holy Spirit lives within
us (Romans 8:9). The Holy Spirit is our helper and will be with us forever.
He is truth. He will teach us and help bring to memory those things that
have been spoken to us through God's Word (John 14:16–17, 26). We
are also told that the world cannot receive the Holy Spirit because they
neither see nor know Him.

It was the Holy Spirit speaking to our hearts and minds, our own
spirit, before we even knew there was a Holy Spirit, that declared to us
that we were not right with God, that we were guilty of rebellion and
disbelief. The Holy Spirit impressed with a sense of guilt our need to
accept Christ's righteousness to save us from the judgment of the evil
within us and without.

You need to know something else about the Holy Spirit: He is the Helper. "Helper" means you are involved in the work of your new life in Christ. It is by His power that this is accomplished, but you must join in and trust His instruction to be the friend that God meant you to be from the beginning of time.

I think there is a myth that as we turn over our sorrows, burdens, hurts, wounds, and lives to Christ, all those things will magically disappear into a meadow of sunshine, flowers, and pots of gold.

Being who God meant us to be is a process. It took time for us to be where we are; it will take time to get where we are going in God's plan for us. We will still need to do the work to reach the goal that God has for us. The difference is that now we are empowered by the supernatural help of His Holy Spirit. We can't do it alone, and He won't do it without us. It was never meant to be that way. In the beginning it was God who brought us beside Him in the garden; we separated ourselves from Him.

> "Come to me, all who labor and are heavy laden, and I will give you rest. Take my yoke upon you, and learn from me, for I am gentle and lowly in heart, and you will find rest for your souls. For my yoke is easy, and my burden is light" (Matthew 11:28–30 ESV).

Jesus said, take my yoke upon you and learn from me …

The yoke is a large piece of wood shaped to fit an ox or oxen. It is placed upon their shoulders and connected to a load that needs to be pulled. The picture is of Jesus with the yoke upon his shoulders and an empty end of the yoke waiting for me to join in the work. There I stand hunched over in pain and fatigue from the heavy load I bear on my own shoulders. He calls out and tells me to leave my load where I stand and to join Him with His. He tells me, "Come learn from me; I tell you you have been heavy laden with all the wrong things that have made your load more than you can bear. Come join me, for I am compassionate and humble in heart. Join in this with me, and you will find the rest that you so desperately seek. My yoke is easy; you will find working in tandem with me to be easy and a fit that does not cause soreness. You will find that my burden is light when you work side by side with me" (my paraphrase).

This is good, and it is pleasing in the sight of God our Savior, who desires all people to be saved and to come to the knowledge of the truth (1 Timothy 2:3–4 ESV).

If you really want to gain knowledge, you must begin by having respect for the Lord. But foolish people hate wisdom and training (Proverbs 1:7 NIrV).

What is truth? What good is truth?

Knowing the truth will liberate you, give you hope, ease your burdens, set you free from slavery.

Jesus said to him, "I am the way, and the truth, and the life ..." (John 14:6 ESV).

"Sanctify them in the truth; your word is truth" (John 17:17 ESV).

Set us apart as being holy in the truth; Your Word is what is true (my paraphrase of John 17:17).

Jesus prayed to the Father to make us a people set apart from the world as a holy people, made holy only by the truth that we are holy through the covering of Jesus.

"[A]nd you will know the truth, and the truth will set you free" (John 8:32 ESV).

"When the Spirit of truth comes, he will guide you into all the truth, for he will not speak on his own authority, but whatever he hears he will speak, and he will declare to you the things that are to come (John 16:13 ESV).

Chapter 5

The Path to Freedom

I wonder, is there something in your life that haunts you? Something that you try to drown out with drugs, alcohol, or some overindulgent behavior? Or maybe you have been able to bury it so deep that it is no longer in your conscience but it causes an unexplainable nagging unhappiness in your life. Something you don't think God can forgive you for or that you yourself cannot forgive yourself for? Listen to the story of Manasseh in 2 Chronicles 33.

Manasseh was one of the kings of Judah; he was labeled the worst king to have ever reigned over God's people. It is stated in the Bible that he did more evil and caused more bloodshed than the Amorites from whom God took the land of Canaan and gave to the Israelites. He erected altars all over the country to worship pagan gods and led the people of Judah to do more evil than all the nations that God had destroyed before the people of Israel. He even made idols and placed them in the temple that King Solomon had built for the Lord God, where the Lord God had said to David and Solomon, "There I have chosen to put My Name forever." (2 Chronicles 33:7) Manasseh even burned his own sons as offerings to pagan gods. (2 Chronicles 33:6)

The Lord spoke to Manasseh and the people of Judah, but they refused to listen. So the Lord sent the army of Assyria, who captured Manasseh with a hook and bound him with chains and brought him to Babylon. Manasseh, being in great distress, prayed and begged for forgiveness from the Lord. He humbled himself greatly before the Lord, and the Lord had pity on him. Because he humbled himself and repented, the Lord sent him back to Judah and his kingdom.

Manasseh did a complete 180-degree turn and took all the foreign gods and removed the idols from the temple of God. He removed all the altars he had built and threw them outside the city. He also rebuilt the altars of the Lord and offered peace offerings and thanksgiving offerings unto the Lord. He commanded all of Judah to serve the Lord God of Israel.

So you see, there is nothing that the Lord God will not forgive if you humble yourself and bow down to Him, pray to Him, and ask for forgiveness from your heart. Turn to Him with all your heart, and He will restore you.

Then do the next right thing.

Jesus went away to pray with the disciples. Taking Peter, James, and John with Him, He went farther into the garden and asked them to keep watch and pray. Jesus went a little farther to pray, as He was greatly grieved over what was to take place next—His arrest and crucifixion. Jesus came back to the disciples to find them asleep (Matthew 26:36–40).

The disciples should have been praying during Jesus's greatest hour of need, but they fell asleep. When they realized what they had done, they were filled with despair. When we become conscious of something that we have done or of a missed opportunity that is unchangeable, it usually brings about despair. We tend to think, *Well, it's all over now; I really messed that up. What's the use in trying anymore?* If we think that we are the only ones who have experienced that kind of despair, we are sadly mistaken. That experience is quite common. Jesus comes simply and says to us with compassion, "Sleep on; that opportunity is gone forever. Rise up and move on to the next right thing to do." He is telling us to let the past sleep in His loving, forgiving arms and move into the future with Him.

When we experience times like these—and we will—in our despair we will feel unable to lift ourselves up out of them. The disciples had let Jesus down by not watching and praying with Him, but Jesus taking the initiative, came to them and in essence said, "Get up and do the next right thing." The next right thing is to trust God, pray, and be attentive to His will.

Never let past failures defeat your next step. [11]

Be brutally honest about yourself:

> Therefore, confess your sins to one another and pray for one another, that you may be healed. The prayer of a righteous person has great power as it is working (James 5:16 ESV).

Learn to speak the truth about yourself that you might heal:

Dr. Steve Stephens, in his book *The Wounded Warrior*, states, "It's time to unashamedly speak the truth about our wounds."

To admit our wounds is:

to be honest

to be real

to be courageous

to be humble

to be healthy [12]

What wounds are you suffering from?

Dr. Stephens lists nine kinds of wounds:

1) Physical wounds   (disease, injury)
2) Bad choices   (selfish, stupid, or impulsive decision)
3) Verbal wounds   (rejection, ridicule)
4) Social wounds   (humiliated, excluded, or attacked by others)
5) Family wounds   (rejected, disrespected by family)
6) Spiritual wounds   (feel hurt by church, clergy, or God)
7) Financial wounds   (a sense of failure)
8) Occupational wounds   (a sense of unworthy)
9) Emotional wounds   (original wound so buried that it is covered with emotion) [13]

Take some time to ponder this list of wounds. When your wound or wounds are revealed to you, this is the burden, the load that Jesus calls out to you to leave and join Him. This whole endeavor, this compiling of God's Word, my thoughts, and others being led by the Holy Spirit, comes to this point. I, like Jesus, wish and implore you to see that you are carrying things you were not meant to carry and that they are robbing you of the joy of life that you were created for. That life that you were created for can be realized only by taking His offer to leave your burden and join Him in His.

Please listen to me when I say, I believe this book can help many people, but I have no formal education to advise you on what level of help you need, if any. Please, if you are hurting in any way, start your healing by talking to a Christian pastor or counselor.

Words are easy and a dime a dozen, aren't they? This is where so many new Christians start out disillusioned. It sounds easy, but as we try to obey God's instructions, it is sometimes difficult and discouraging. Satan, ourselves, and others are quick to condemn when we fail or falter. Guilt moves in, and we are discouraged to the point of wanting to give up. Don't! Don't give up; God is right there to help you try again.

God had just performed a great miracle through Elijah, proving the one true God was the God of Abraham, Isaac, and Jacob to the king of Israel, Ahab, the congregation standing about, and the 450 prophets of Baal who had failed to light the sacrifice on their altar. The challenge was that Elijah would build an altar and place a sacrifice on it and so would the king and the prophets of Baal. They would call out to their gods, and the one that set fire to the sacrifices would prove to be the true God. King Ahab and the prophets of Baal would go first. After more than half the day spent calling out, shouting, and even cutting themselves, with blood flowing from their bodies onto the sacrifice, there was no answer from their god Baal.

Elijah called the crowd to the altar built for the sacrifice to the God of Israel. He had dug a ditch around it that would hold about six gallons of water. He called to the congregation to fill four large jars with water and pour all the water over the sacrifice and the wood. This was repeated three times. Then Elijah prayed to God and asked the God of Israel to show the people that the God of Israel was the one true God and that Elijah was his servant. God sent down fire from heaven and consumed the sacrifice, the wood, the rock, the ground, and all the water. The people confessed, "The LORD He is God!" Elijah had the people kill all the prophets of Baal. It was a great day for the Lord!

King Ahab went home and told the evil queen what Elijah had done. In her anger she sent word to Elijah promising, "May the gods deal with me, be it ever so severely, if by this time tomorrow I do not make your life like that of one of them." Elijah feared for his life and ran far into the wilderness. He came to a bush, sat under it, and prayed that he might die. "I have had enough LORD. Take my life; I am no better than my ancestors." Then he lay down and fell asleep.

He had just performed a great victory with his God. It didn't get the results he thought it was supposed to. He felt like such a failure. What's the use? I did my best! What more could have been done? The king saw with his own two eyes that you are the one true God, and for that they want to hunt me down and kill me! I'm done! I give up! Take my life, Lord! I give up! (1 Kings 18:20–40, 19:1–4)

> And he lay down and slept under a broom tree. And behold, an angel touched him and said to him, "Arise and eat" (1Kings 19: 5 ESV).

The angel did not give Elijah some great vision, nor did he enlighten him to what God's purpose was in the great miracle that he had just performed with God. The angel didn't do anything extraordinary; he simply told Elijah to get up and eat. If we were never depressed, then we would not be alive; depression is part of life. If we were not capable of depression, how could we experience the fulfillment of happiness? There are situations in life that are designed to depress, such as the loss of a loved one. There are also situations that bring about joy and happiness, such as the birth of a new baby in the family. There are so many levels of joy and depression in between. Always take into consideration your ability to withstand depression.

When God's Holy Spirit speaks to us, it is not in visions of grandeur, but in the ordinary things in life. When we are depressed, we are inclined to turn away from the ordinary simple little things in life, things that we would not expect God to be involved in. When God gets involved in our depression, His Holy Spirit will inspire us to do the most natural simple things like He did with Elijah: "Get up and eat." When we obey, we see that His inspiration is the introductory step against depression. Our first step must be taken in the inspiration of God. If we try to do things just to conquer our depression, we will only cover over it and cause it to deepen. However, when we heed the nudging of God's Holy Spirit to do something, the minute we obey, the depression is gone. As soon as we arise and obey, we are back in purpose with God. [14]

Don't give up. Get some rest, and then get up and be nourished, physically and spiritually.

> If he stumbles, he's not down for long; GOD has a grip
> on his hand (Psalm 37:24 MSG).

> "God is striding ahead of you. He's right there with you.
> He won't let you down; he won't leave you. Don't be
> intimidated. Don't worry" (Deuteronomy 31:8 MSG).

Some people are able to leave their burdens, their pain, and their baggage behind, walk away, and never turn back. Those people are blessed with the faith and self-discipline to take God's word for it and accomplish their goal. Others can lay the burdens down, take two steps away, and turn around and reach to pick them up again. They have the desire but lack the confidence, faith, and discipline to accomplish their goal. A mentor is needed to lead and encourage them down the right path. Then there are those whose wounds and pain are so deep and embedded that professional help is needed to separate them from their very being. This situation brings to mind a summer when I spent time on my uncle's farm helping him mend the barbed-wire fence in one of his fields. Whenever a tree happened to be within the fence line, farmers would nail the barbed wire to the tree. Eventually, the tree would grow over the barbed wire and the wire would become part of the tree. Our wounds and pain, if they are not addressed, become part of our very being. They become so embedded in us that it seems impossible to separate the two. Don't give up—with God nothing is impossible. Let me encourage you to seek Christian professional help. Yes, I said Christian professional help. God works through people, and you want a professional who knows how to help and has the wisdom to use God's principles to lead you to the healing you need.

I do live in the world. But I don't fight my battles the way the people of the world do. The weapons I fight with are not the weapons the world uses. In fact, it is just the opposite. My weapons have the power of God to destroy the camps of the enemy. I destroy every claim and every reason that keeps people from knowing God. I keep every thought under control in order to make it obey Christ. Until you have obeyed completely, I will be ready to punish you every time you don't obey (2 Corinthians 10:3–6 NIrV).

Finally, let the Lord make you strong. Depend on his mighty power. Put on all of God's armor. Then you can stand firm against the devil's evil plans. Our fight is not against human beings. It is against the rulers, the authorities and the powers of this dark world. It is against the spiritual forces of evil in the heavenly world. So put on all of God's armor. Evil days will come. But you will be able to stand up to anything. And after you have done everything you can, you will still be standing. So stand firm. Put the belt of truth around your waist. Put the armor of godliness on your chest. Wear on your feet what will prepare you to tell the good news of peace. Also, pick up the shield of faith. With it you can put out all of the flaming arrows of the evil one. Put on the helmet of salvation. And take the sword of the Holy Spirit. The sword is God's word. At all times, pray by the power of the Spirit. Pray all kinds of prayers. Be watchful, so that you can pray. Always keep on praying for all of God's people (Ephesians 6:10–18 NIrV).

And that about wraps it up. God is strong, and he wants you strong. So take everything the Master has set out for you, well-made weapons of the best materials. And put them to use so you will be able to stand up to everything the Devil throws your way. This is no afternoon athletic contest that we'll walk away from and forget about in a couple of hours. This is for keeps, a life-or-death fight to the finish against the Devil and all his angels. Be prepared. You're up against far more than you can handle on your own. Take all the help you can get, every weapon God has issued, so that when it's all over but the shouting you'll still be on your feet. Truth, righteousness, peace, faith, and salvation are more than words. Learn how to apply them. You'll need them throughout your life. God's Word is an indispensable weapon. In the same way, prayer is essential in this ongoing warfare. Pray hard and long. Pray for your brothers and sisters. Keep your eyes open. Keep each other's spirits up so that no one falls behind or drops out (Ephesians 6:10–18 MSG).

You must pray, read the Bible, and obey!

Because Christ is in you, you are no longer a slave of the flesh. You are now a servant of the Holy Spirit, which lives in you.

What is the difference between a slave and a servant? As a slave you are controlled by an outside force; as a servant you work from free will.

You must change the way you think!

For as he thinks in his heart, so is he (Proverbs 23:7a KJV).

For those who live according to the flesh set their minds on the things of the flesh, but those who live according to the Spirit set their minds on the things of the Spirit. For to set the mind on the flesh is death, but to set the mind on the Spirit is life and peace (Romans 8:5–6 ESV).

Don't live under the control of your sinful nature. If you do, you will think about what your sinful nature wants. Live under the control of the Holy Spirit. If you do, you will think about what the Spirit wants. The way a sinful person thinks leads to death. But the mind controlled by the Spirit brings life and peace (Romans 8:5–6 NIrV).

Those who think they can do it on their own end up obsessed with measuring their own moral muscle but never get around to exercising it in real life. Those who trust God's action in them find that God's Spirit is in them— living and breathing God! Obsession with self in these matters is a dead end; attention to God leads us out into the open, into a spacious, free life. Focusing on the self is the opposite of focusing on God. Anyone completely absorbed in self ignores God, ends up thinking more about self than God. That person ignores who God is and what he is doing. And God isn't pleased at being ignored. But if God himself has taken up residence in your life, you can hardly be thinking more of yourself than of him. Anyone, of course, who has not welcomed this invisible but clearly present God, the Spirit of Christ, won't know what we're talking about. But for you who welcome him, in whom he dwells— even though you still experience all the limitations of sin — you yourself experience life on God's terms. It stands to reason, doesn't it, that if the alive-and-present God who raised Jesus from the dead moves into your life, he'll do the same thing in you that he did in Jesus, bringing you alive to himself? When God lives and breathes in you (and he does, as surely as he did in Jesus), you are delivered from that dead life. With his Spirit living in you, your body will be as alive as Christ's! So don't you see that we don't owe this old do-it-yourself life one red cent. There's nothing in it for us, nothing at all. The best thing to do is give it a decent burial and get on with your new life. God's Spirit beckons. There are things to do and places to go! This resurrection life you received from God is not a timid, grave-tending life. It's adventurously expectant, greeting God with a childlike "What's next, Papa?" God's Spirit touches our spirits and confirms who we really are. We know who he is, and we know who we are: Father and children. And we know we are going to get what's coming to us — an unbelievable inheritance! We go through exactly what Christ goes through. If we go through the hard times with him, then we're certainly going to go through the good times with him! (Romans 8:5–17 MSG)

Don't you see the power that is within you because God's Holy Spirit lives within you?

He will not force you. You must surrender your will to Him to receive healing and the spirit-filled life that God has for you.

Then he said, "This is GOD's Message to Zerubbabel: 'You can't force these things. They only come about through my Spirit,' says GOD-of-the-Angel-Armies'" (Zechariah 4:6 MSG).

So he said to me, "A message came to Zerubbabel from the Lord. He said, 'Your strength will not get my temple rebuilt. Your power will not do it either. Only the power of my Spirit will do it,' says the Lord who rules over all'" (Zechariah 4:6 NIrV).

Quit talking about it and do it!

"But the things that come out of the mouth come from the heart. Those are the things that make you 'unclean.' Evil thoughts come out of the heart. So do murder, adultery, and other sexual sins. And so do stealing, false witness, and telling lies about others" (Matthew 15:18–19 NIrV).

All of us get tripped up in many ways. Suppose someone is never wrong in what he says. Then he is a perfect man. He is able to keep his whole body under control.

We put a bit in the mouth of a horse to make it obey us. We can control the whole animal with it. And how about ships? They are very big. They are driven along by strong winds. But they are steered by a very small rudder. It makes them go where the captain wants to go. In the same way, the tongue is a small part of the body. But it brags a lot. Think about how a small spark can set a big forest on fire. The tongue also is a fire. The tongue is the most evil part of the body. It pollutes the whole person. It sets a person's whole way of life on fire. And the tongue is set on fire by hell. People have controlled all kinds of animals, birds, reptiles and creatures of the sea. They still control them. But no one can control the tongue. It is an evil thing that never rests. It is full of deadly poison. With our tongues we praise our Lord and Father. With our tongues we call down curses on people. We do it even though they have been created to be like God. Praise and cursing come out of the same mouth. My brothers and sisters, it shouldn't be that way. Can fresh water and salt water flow out of the same spring? My brothers and sisters, can a fig tree bear olives? Can a grapevine bear figs? Of course not. And a saltwater spring can't produce fresh water either. Are any of you wise and understanding? You should show it by living a good life. Wise people aren't proud when they do good works. But suppose your hearts are jealous and bitter. Suppose you are concerned only about getting ahead. Don't brag about it. Don't say no to the truth. Wisdom like that doesn't come down from heaven. It belongs to the earth. It doesn't come from the Holy Spirit. It comes from the devil. Are you jealous? Are you concerned only about getting ahead? Then your life will be a mess. You will be doing all kinds of evil things. But the wisdom that comes from heaven is pure. That's the most important thing about it. And that's not all. It also loves peace. It thinks about others. It obeys. It is full of mercy and good fruit. It is fair. It doesn't pretend to be what it is not. Those who make peace should plant peace like a seed. If they do, it will produce a crop of right living (James 3:2–18 NIrV).

Obey without question and earthly reasoning to the one you can trust! Who can you trust—doctors, counselors, family, friends, spouses? Will they, or can they, even be there always, at any given moment? Only God can do that!

Let your conduct be without covetousness; be content with such things as you have. For He Himself has said, "I will never leave you nor forsake you" (Hebrews 13:5 NKJV).

"Be strong and courageous. Do not fear or be in dread of them, for it is the LORD your God who goes with you. He will not leave you or forsake you" (Deuteronomy 31:6 ESV).

Chapter 6

God and Reconciliation

Ever since Adam and Eve rebelled against God and were cast from the perfect garden that He had made for them to experience life together, an environment where God walked and talked with them daily, God has been reconciling humanity to Himself. You cannot have the relationship God intended without being reconciled to Him. God's Word teaches us that we also must seek reconciliation with our brothers in order to have a right relationship with God.

Jacob and Esau were brothers. Jacob cheated and stole Esau's birthright from him by taking advantage of his brother in his moment of need and weakness. Jacob lied to his father as well to receive Esau's blessing from his father. Esau, angry at his brother, sought to kill Jacob. Jacob's mother, Rebekah, warned him and sent him to live with her brother Laban. After Jacob had worked twenty years for Laban, his now father-in-law, God told Jacob to return and to reconcile with his brother, Esau. Fearing for his life right up to the embrace of Esau, happy to see his brother, Jacob was obedient to God and reconciled with his brother. Jacob could not grow in his relationship with God until he had reconciled with his brother (Genesis 25:29–34; 27:1–29, 41–45; 31:38–41; 32:9–11; 33:1–4).

Joseph, his father's favorite son, was hated by all of his brothers. They hated that their father loved him more and treated him better than he treated them. Joseph compounded the problem by telling them about a dream in which they all bowed down to him.

Joseph was sent by his father to check on his brothers as they were tending to their father's flock. When the brothers saw him coming from far away, they plotted to kill Joseph. Judah convinced them not to kill him but to sell him to a band of Ishmaelites, who in turn sold him as a slave in Egypt.

Joseph was blessed by God, even through his many hardships, and became second in command only to the pharaoh of Egypt. A seven-year famine brought Joseph's brothers to him seeking to buy food to take back to their father and younger brother back home. They did not recognize Joseph because they thought he was dead, but Joseph recognized them. God brought them together so that Joseph might reconcile with his brothers. When Joseph revealed himself to his brothers, they feared for their lives. Joseph calmed their fears and told them not to be afraid, that he forgave them and that what they meant for evil God had used as good that they and many people might be saved through this time of famine (Genesis 37:3–28; 39-45:8; 50:15-21).

It doesn't matter if we are the victim or the offender ... we must seek reconciliation if we wish to have a right relationship with God. If we are the victim, we are to offer forgiveness freely to the one who offended, whether they ask or not. If we are the offender, we are to beg forgiveness from the one we offended and do whatever we can to make our relationship right with that person:

> 'Forgive us our sins, *just as we also have forgiven* those who sin against us' (emphasis mine; Matthew 6:12 NIrV).

> "Forgive people when they sin against you. If you do, your Father who is in heaven will also forgive you. But if you do not forgive people their sins, your Father will not forgive your sins" (Matthew 6: 14–15 NIrV).

> "In prayer there is a connection between what God does and what you do. You can't get forgiveness from God, for instance, without also forgiving others. If you refuse to do your part, you cut yourself off from God's part" (Matthew 6:14–15 MSG).

> "This is how I want you to conduct yourself in these matters. If you enter your place of worship and, about

to make an offering, you suddenly remember a grudge a friend has against you, abandon your offering, leave immediately, go to this friend and make things right. Then and only then, come back and work things out with God" (Matthew 5:23–24 MSG).

God's Word is saying, "Don't expect forgiveness from me if you can't give forgiveness to your fellow man! Don't you dare come before me worshiping and bringing gifts to me when you know someone is offended by something you have done! Go and make it right between yourselves, and then come back and let us celebrate together."

If you listen, God will send you on journeys to be reconciled and to reconcile.

Joseph's time in prison

Joseph was handsome in form and appearance. And after a time his master's wife cast her eyes on Joseph and said, "Lie with me." But he refused and said to his master's wife, "Behold, because of me my master has no concern about anything in the house, and he has put everything that he has in my charge. He is not greater in this house than I am, nor has he kept back anything from me except you, because you are his wife. How then can I do this great wickedness and sin against God?" And as she spoke to Joseph day after day, he would not listen to her, to lie beside her or to be with her. But one day, when he went into the house to do his work and none of the men of the house was there in the house, she caught him by his garment, saying, "Lie with me." But he left his garment in her hand and fled and got out of the house. And as soon as she saw that he had left his garment in her hand and had fled out of the house, she called to the men of her household and said to them, "See, he has brought among us a Hebrew to laugh at us. He came in to me to lie with me, and I cried out with a loud voice. And as soon as he heard that I lifted up my voice and cried out, he left his garment beside me and fled and got out of the house." Then she laid up his garment by her until his master came home, and she told him the same story, saying, "The Hebrew servant, whom you have brought among us, came in to me to laugh at me. But as soon as I lifted up my voice and cried, he left his garment beside me and fled out of the house." As soon as his master heard the words that his wife spoke to him, "This is the way your servant treated me," his anger was kindled. And Joseph's master took him and put him into the prison, the place where the king's prisoners were confined, and he was there in prison. But the LORD was with Joseph and showed him steadfast love and gave him favor in the sight of the keeper of the prison (Genesis 39:6b–21 ESV).

Randy Frazee put together a church curriculum called "The Story." In it, Randy talks about the lower story and the upper story of life. We, in the lower story, have our ideas and rules about life, and we fortify them with reasons of tangible expediencies and common sense. In the upper story is God! God has ideas and rules that are so high above our ability to comprehend, that because of our inability to do such, we simply think He is not involved because His actions do not conform to our ideas and rules of life. They even seem to contradict what we perceive God to be like. So here we see Joseph refusing to sin against God and running from the grasp of his master's wife. Joseph is thrown into prison! How is that right? How is that fair? Does God reward Joseph for honoring Him by abandoning Joseph? We get so tied up in our lower story and how we think God should respond to what is happening in our lives that we miss what God is doing in the upper story. We read through that whole story, and shout out so loudly, "How unfair! How unjust! Where is God?" that we miss the soft whisper of God in that last verse. "But the Lord was with Joseph and showed him steadfast love and gave him favor in the sight of the keeper of the prison." God never leaves us no matter where circumstance may put us.

Did you ever have one of those moments when you did what was right and you wound up suffering for it?

How do you think Joseph was able to keep from being bitter through this great injustice? Had Joseph learned to accept his circumstances, whatever they may be?

Listen to what Paul has to say:

> I'm not saying that because I need anything. I have learned to be content no matter what happens to me. I know what it's like not to have what I need. I also know what it's like to have more than I need. I have learned the secret of being content no matter what happens. I am content whether I am well fed or hungry. I am content whether I have more than enough or not enough. I can do everything by the power of Christ. He gives me strength (Philippians 4:11–13 NIrV).

Somehow we need to learn to be content. We need to realize that God is in control, even if it does not seem so. We need to realize that God is personally involved with our lives and knows our every thought, desire, need, joy, and physical and emotional pain. God has plans for us.

> "For I know the plans I have for you, declares the LORD, plans for welfare and not for evil, to give you a future and a hope" (Jeremiah 29:11 ESV).

Where do you see yourself in this Word of God?

> GOD, investigate my life; get all the facts firsthand. I'm an open book to you; even from a distance, you know what I'm thinking. You know when I leave and when I get back; I'm never out of your sight. You know everything I'm going to say before I start the first sentence. I look behind me and you're there, then up ahead and you're there, too—your reassuring presence, coming and going. This is too much, too wonderful— I can't take it all in! Is there anyplace I can go to avoid your Spirit? to be out of your sight? If I climb to the sky, you're there! If I go

underground, you're there! If I flew on morning's wings to the far western horizon, You'd find me in a minute — you're already there waiting! Then I said to myself, "Oh, he even sees me in the dark! At night I'm immersed in the light!" It's a fact: darkness isn't dark to you; night and day, darkness and light, they're all the same to you. Oh yes, you shaped me first inside, then out; you formed me in my mother's womb. I thank you, High God— you're breathtaking! Body and soul, I am marvelously made! I worship in adoration— what a creation! You know me inside and out, you know every bone in my body; You know exactly how I was made, bit by bit, how I was sculpted from nothing into something. Like an open book, you watched me grow from conception to birth; all the stages of my life were spread out before you, the days of my life all prepared before I'd even lived one day. Your thoughts— how rare, how beautiful! God, I'll never comprehend them! I couldn't even begin to count them— any more than I could count the sand of the sea. Oh, let me rise in the morning and live always with you! (Psalm 139:1–18 MSG)

Is there anything you can hide from God? What do you have to do to find God?

"When you come looking for me, you'll find me. "Yes, when you get serious about finding me and want it more than anything else, I'll make sure you won't be disappointed." GOD's Decree".. I'll turn things around for you. I'll bring you back from all the countries into which I drove you"-GOD's Decree – "bring you home to the place from which I sent you off into exile. You can count on it (Jeremiah 29:13–14 MSG).

Have you, like Israel and Judah, turned your back on God? Do you now find yourself carried off in exile to a sinful place like Babylon?

"Then you will call upon me and come and pray to
me, and I will hear you. You will seek me and find me,
when you seek me with all your heart" (Jeremiah 29:12–
13 ESV).

I kneel at the base of my bed to pray, "How are You doing, Father?"
What a strange thing to ask of God. But really, how is He doing; how is
He handling all this mess in His heart?

I came home from work one day to hear my wife tell me our oldest
son was very upset because one of his friends was found dead in his jail
cell that morning with no apparent cause. I was told he was riding in a car
with his girlfriend and was pulled over by the police; he had warrants for
failure to pay child support. For some stupid reason he decided to run. He
was caught and arrested on suspicion of driving with a suspended license.

Our son brought his friend to Bible study one Sunday; he told me
while his friend was in Texas he had attended his grandmother's church
and felt welcome there. Our church wasn't what he was looking for, so
our son would take him to Faith Church, where he went. They were
going quite often, sometimes twice a week. Our son was upset; his friend
had been turning his life around and had been working on his relationship
with God. How sad! How battle-torn and weary his friend must have
been.

How are You doing, Father? I know we're made in Your image! Surely
You feel the pain as well. After all, you sighed with your only Son over
Jerusalem. "Jerusalem, Jerusalem ... How often would I have gathered
your children together as a hen gathers her brood under her wings"
(Matthew 23:37). How are You doing, Father? How heavy the grief must
be in Your heart! The loss of one weary soldier pulls me down pressed
against the grave of grief. Even You being God—how do You bear it?
There is a limit that You have set from the foundation of the Earth, a
weight at which You say, "Stop! No more!" And Your Son breaks through
the clouds to set things right. How are You doing, Father? How much
longer?

Thank you, Father, for the weary, battle-torn soldier that found him, dazed and confused, bleeding from his wounds and helped him to Your camp. Give Your warriors strength.

Abraham had two sons, one from a slave woman and one from a free woman (Galatians 4:22).

Paul is speaking about the relationship between the natural and the spiritual. The transforming of the natural into the spiritual can be done only through sacrifice. Without doing so, one will live a double life. It was not God's perfect will that the natural be sacrificed, but it became His permissive will. His perfect will was that the natural would be changed to the spiritual through obedience. Because of our sin and rebellion, it became necessary to sacrifice the natural.

Abraham had to offer up Ishmael, the natural-born son of the slave, before he could offer up Isaac, the son of the free woman born of a miracle of God (Genesis 16:1–4; 21:1–3, 10–12; 22:2–12). Are you trying to offer spiritual sacrifices to God without having sacrificed your natural self? We cannot offer spiritual sacrifices to God until we have offered our natural selves, our bodies as a living sacrifice. Being sanctified means more than just being free from sin; it means calculated and predetermined commitment of myself, my all, my everything, absolutely nothing held back from the God of my salvation … no matter what the cost.

If we refuse to sacrifice the natural life to the spiritual life, the natural will counteract, neutralize, and work against the life of Jesus within us, just as Ishmael did to Isaac. This will always be the outcome of the undisciplined spiritual nature. The problem comes when we willfully refuse to discipline ourselves completely—mentally, morally, and physically. We seem to want to blame our actions on our parents: "I was not taught to be disciplined when I was a growing up." Well, you're grown up now, so take responsibility for yourself and discipline yourself; if you don't, it will be the undoing of your personal life for God.

God is not actively working in our natural life when we submit to and indulge it. As soon as we send it to the desert as Abraham did with Ishmael, and determine to let it be in God's care, then God will walk with us. He will bless us and fulfill all His promises for the natural as well. [15]

If we are to grow spiritually, we must sacrifice the nature of our natural self … our flesh … those things that appeal to our natural senses.

Abraham had been promised a son by God. After a time, Sarah, who was unable to conceive and was well beyond childbearing age, convinced her husband, Abraham, to go into her maid Hagar, so that she might conceive a son for him. Abraham and Sarah tried to fulfill God's promise the natural way, and Ishmael (representing the natural) was born to them through Hagar. That was not what God had in mind. God's thoughts and ways are spiritual; they are higher than our thoughts and ways. God, through the power of His Spirit, opened up the womb of Sarah, and she conceived Isaac (representing the spiritual).

Ishmael began to mock and make fun of Isaac, so Ishmael and his mother were sent away so that Isaac could grow and inherit the promises made to Abraham. So it is with us: we must send away our natural thoughts and self-gratifying ways that mock the way of God if we are to grow spiritually and inherit the promises that God has made to us through the work of His Son, Jesus. If we do not do this, then the natural life will always antagonize and mock the spiritual life of Jesus within us. Discipline is the means to bring the natural under control, and discipline will bring spiritual growth.

If you are tired of being controlled by your flesh, natural senses, addictions, depression, any type of ungodly lifestyle, or you wish to have a closer walk with God, you must change! God will not do it without your participation. You must *desire* change, you must be *determined* to change, and you must *discipline* yourself to change.

You will not reach your full potential without these three *d*'s coupled with the power of the Holy Spirit! Your part is the possession of the three *d*'s, bringing about obedience through the supernatural power of the Holy Spirit, culminating in a closer walk and relationship with Jesus and God our Father.

Chapter 7

Three—Dimensional Change

I want to go back to something I shared earlier.

First, if we belong to the kingdom by our acceptance of what Jesus has done for us, He will place a *desire* in our hearts to learn, to know, to experience all that we can grasp about our heavenly Father and His Son—our King, our priest, our brother, Jesus Christ.

By faith we must *determine* to fight through all obstacles to place God first in *all things*—to search His Word, to learn who He is and what He expects of us, to determine to make our relationship with God above all others.

Through the power of the Holy Spirit we must *discipline* ourselves to be obedient to all that God's Word teaches us.

My hope is that as you read the first part of this book you came to recognize the great gift of love sent on our behalf through Jesus, the only way to God the Father. If you did and have accepted Christ as your Savior, then the desire in your heart, mind, and soul is to know the blessings of the friendship of Jesus, God the Father, and His kingdom.

Now, some people may say, I have accepted Christ as my Savior, but I don't seem to have that desire in my heart, nor do I feel like anything has changed in my life. That is not an altogether uncommon feeling, but it should cause a sincere searching and evaluation of your decision and acceptance of Christ as your Savior. Many prominent Christians through history have experienced that same feeling, and it led them to search for that missing desire, peace of knowing, and full trust in Jesus the Christ.

John Bunyan, who authored the classic *The Pilgrim's Progress*, being convicted of his sins, tried to work his way through righteousness by being a godly man. After hearing some women discussing Scripture they were studying, John was moved to put his trust in the Lord Jesus for salvation and not his own works. [16]

Charlotte Elliott, who wrote the famous hymn "Just as I Am," although her father and brother were ministers and her grandfather was the famous preacher Henry Venn, admitted she felt alienated from God. After Dr. Caesar Malan, a minister and family friend, questioned her about her faith, she later said, "I wish to be saved; I just don't know how to do that." Dr. Malan simply stated, "Come just as you are." The words spoke volumes to her, and there was nothing she could do but give what she was at that moment to Christ and trust in Him. [17]

Dawson Trotman was the leader of the Christian Endeavor Society at Lomita Presbyterian Church, but he was living a double life—one with alcohol and gambling. After hitting rock bottom, he went back to his church and became interested in the Scripture memorization contest, learning twenty verses. Those verses began to speak to him about eternal life and receiving Jesus. Dawson simply told God, "Whatever it takes to acquire Jesus, I wish to do now."

Dawson committed his life to Christ and joined a personal evangelism group. He went on to found the Minute Men, which was later renamed the Navigators. Billy Graham, in 1950, approached Dawson with the task of creating a follow-up curriculum for converts from the crusades. [18]

Charles Wesley; John Wesley, known for leading revival in the Church of England and founding the Methodist Church; and George Whitefield, who helped spread the Great Awakening in Britain and the American colonies, began a Christian group at Oxford University focusing on religious self-discipline, working their way for salvation. One of the original founders of the Christian group, William Morgan, drove himself to madness and eventually lost his life trying to acquire perfection through self-discipline.

George Whitefield, near madness and so weak he lay in his bed for seven weeks, had hit bottom trying to earn his salvation. George said that God removed the burden of salvation by self-disciplined works and now claimed the gift of His Son by faith.

It was three years later before the Wesleys claimed salvation by faith and not by their own works. [19]

David Brainerd, a missionary to the Indians of Massachusetts, New Jersey, and Pennsylvania, and a close friend of the famous preacher Jonathan Edwards, had misconceptions about salvation as well. David greatly admired his older brother and wanted to follow in his footsteps as a minister. David did not agree with many of the Bible's doctrines and disliked the fact that he could do nothing to commend himself to God through his own works.

Although studying for the ministry, David was not even a church member. In order to be a member, one had to have an assurance of salvation, and he did not. One Friday morning while he was walking in the forest, he realized that he was spiritually lost. He realized that all of his religious plans and works in no way obligated God to grant him with saving grace. Two days later as he walked through that same forest, God graciously answered his searching by filling his heart with the wisdom of salvation by faith—through the righteousness of Christ and what He had done on the cross. God's Spirit impressed upon his heart that there was nothing that we can do but accept his gift of sacrifice on our behalf. [20]

John Sung was born to a Methodist minister in southeast China. In a great revival he attended at age nine, he gave his life to Jesus. He committed his time to helping his father and studying for evangelism. At the age of eighteen he had a dream that he would be a great evangelist.

John went to America to study at Ohio Wesleyan University; then he went on to Ohio State University, where he earned a PhD in chemistry. He went to Union Theological Seminary in New York City but felt his faith in Jesus slipping away as a result of his studies in rationalism, Taoism, and Buddhism.

At an evangelistic service John heard a fifteen-year-old girl read from the Scriptures with such conviction and passion that it stirred a deep desire within him to have such faith and power that was in this girl, such as he had had at one time. Later while reading in Luke 23 of the death of Jesus, he was moved to a deep repentance as he was convinced by the Spirit that his sins were indeed forgiven.

For the next fifteen years John was an effective evangelist in China and Southeast Asia. His preaching centered on repentance and the cross of Jesus as the only hope for salvation. [21]

William Grimshaw, who stated he was, in his own words, "as vile as the worst," saw no concerns in the way he lived and the profession of ministry that he chose. He went on to be ordained as a minister in the Church of England. After losing his wife he went into deep depression and sent his two children away to live with relatives. A traveling preacher at about the same time begun to chide him for his views of salvation. He told him, "You do not believe in the Lord Jesus; your foundation is on sand." Grimshaw could not get the words, "your foundation is on sand" out of his mind.

While visiting a friend, he was led by the Spirit of God to a book lying on the table. He took the book home and began to read. He was confronted by the author's question, "Will you trust your own righteousness, or in repentance, accept the righteousness of Christ alone by the grace of God?" [22]

William Grimshaw got it! God had opened his eyes to the understanding that salvation was a gift of God's grace, the work of His Son. John Bunyan, Charlotte Elliott, Dawson Trotman, Charles and John Wesley, George Whitefield, David Brainerd, John Sung, and William Grimshaw all had the misconception that there was something in their power, something that they could do to achieve God's grace. They believed they had to make themselves worthy of God's grace. Oh, what a change it will make in your life when you realize that you *are not* worthy, *nor can* you make yourself to be worthy. *It is God's gift!*

Each of these people came to a crisis of faith. Each one was brought to some form of the question, "Whom will you trust?" Will you trust in what you are doing as the way to salvation, or will you admit to the futility of your works? Will you trust God to solve the problem of your sins, remove them from you, and place them on His Son Jesus?

James Kennedy believed in God and assumed he was a Christian. For James, his crisis of faith came when he woke up one morning with a hangover and the radio was broadcasting a message from Dr. Donald Grey Barnhouse of the Tenth Presbyterian Church in Philadelphia. The question was asked, " If you were to die today and be confronted by God and He asked you, 'What right do you have to enter Heaven?' how would you respond?" He was shocked and could not find an answer. He realized he had no right and gave his life to Christ. [23]

Have you come to your crisis of faith? Can you answer the question, "What right do you have to enter My heaven?" If you have come, and you can answer, then trust that God has forgiven you of your sins, has brought you into His kingdom, made you a member of His family, and will grant you the *desire*. So if we have the *desire* to know, then how do we exercise that *desire*? Through faith! Through faith we have accepted God's promise that we are saved because of the sacrifice and payment made by Christ on the cross. It's not a blind faith; it is a faith, a confidence, a knowing inside of me that all God has done and all God says He will accomplish, has happened and will happen. It is that faith, that confidence, that knowing inside of me that convinces me that the Bible is God's holy Word and He promises me that if I accept the sacrifice of Jesus on my behalf, I am saved (Romans 10:9). He promises me that if I search for Him with all my heart, I will find Him (Jeremiah 29:13) and if I ask Him He will give to me all that I need (Luke 11:9–10).

Now through that faith we must *determine* to be obedient to God's Word, to fulfill that desire that was placed in our heart when we accepted Christ and the new life He has for us.

What does it mean when we *determine* to be obedient to God's Word? It means we have thought, reasoned, and disputed with ourselves about what God expects of us and the new life He has to show us. It means we have settled the dispute and we have decided to take God up on His promise of a new life right now, at this very moment. We are *determined* to be obedient to His Word.

How can we be obedient? By the power of the Holy Spirit through *discipline*. Remember the Holy Spirit is our helper (John 14:16–17). He will be our trainer, our mentor, and our coach. He will train us to control the natural desires and thoughts of our mind through the power, knowledge, and wisdom given to Him by God the Father. Through a series of spiritual disciplines and exercises, the Holy Spirit will bring us to a closer communion with Jesus and our Father God.

Remember, these disciplines are meant to bring us to a closer relationship with God. Disciplines *do not bring* salvation; only our acceptance of what Christ accomplished on the cross on our behalf brings us salvation!

I want to examine these spiritual disciplines and exercises at this point. Some of these disciplines seem to be common in the sense that they are spoken often in church settings; some are not used at all or are used but without much depth. The book *Celebration of Discipline* by Richard J. Foster is an excellent study of spiritual disciplines. The list of disciplines that I use is for the most part from that book. I highly recommend reading his book, as he goes into more detail than I. Here is the list I will use:

Personal Disciplines, one-on-one with the Lord
1) Prayer
2) Obedience
3) Solitude
4) Study
5) Meditation
6) Fasting

Personal Disciplines, shared one-on-one with the Lord as well as directed outward
1) Humility
2) Patience
3) Simplicity
4) Submission
5) Service

Personal Disciplines, in various group settings
1) Worship
2) Fellowship
3) Confession
4) Guidance
5) Celebration

Chapter 8

Personal Disciplines: One-on-One with the Lord

The Discipline of Prayer

I put prayer first because prayer is our communication with God. There is much to be said about communication with God through prayer; it needs to start simple and personal. There are times when we need to spend much time in prayer, and there will be times when we will pray in group settings and for others. There will be times when the Holy Spirit will nudge us to stop and just say hi to God and ask Him what's on His mind at that moment. Sometimes we need to take a moment to kneel and just thank God for being who He is or for whatever comes to your heart. Prayer is just like talking to your best friend.

You need to discipline yourself to set aside prayer time. In Daniel 6:10 we see that Daniel would pray three times a day. David in Psalm 55:17 speaks of uttering his complaints to God morning, noon, and evening and says he knows God hears him. Many times in the New Testament we see Jesus slipping away in the morning and evening to pray alone to the Father. You need to discipline yourself to open your day talking to your heavenly Father and close the day thanking Him for another day and for rest. Tell Him how your day went; ask for help where it's needed. Ask Him where you can give help to others and to open your eyes to understand the opportunities He sets before you.

In Luke 18:1–8, Jesus tells a parable, a story that He uses to teach us to never cease praying, never to give up, not to lose heart. He says there was a judge who could care less what God thought about anything, nor could he care less about other people's needs or concerns unless it was to his advantage. In this judge's district was a poor widow woman who came before him asking that he give her justice against an adversary who was causing her grief. At first he would not grant her justice. After a while, though, he said to himself, "Even though I could care less what is right in the eyes of God or the fact that this poor widow woman has been mistreated or not, I will give her justice just to stop her from continually annoying me with her cry for justice." Then Jesus responds, "How much more will the Heavenly Father give justice to His own who pray to Him day and night?" Because God loves us and cares about us, He will give justice to those who seek His help with perseverance (my paraphrase).

Paul, as well, in 1 Thessalonians 5:17, tells us to pray without ceasing. So never give up praying. Don't be discouraged by the circumstances; keep praying, knowing all the while that God hears you.

We need to discipline ourselves to get in the habit of setting aside those times to be in our closet, so to speak, as Jesus stated in Matthew 6:6, where all our attention can be devoted to conversation with God our Father. The location is not as important as the need for it to be a place of solitude. Daniel prayed in the upper chamber of his house (Daniel 6:10). Peter went up to the housetop to pray (Acts 10:9). In Mark 1:35, Jesus went to a desolate place to pray. In Matthew 26:36, Jesus went to the garden of Gethsemane to pray. In Matthew 14:23, Jesus went up on the mountain to pray. Seek a place with no distractions to be alone with God the Father.

This discipline of prayer is most important! I do not see any other way to grow your relationship with the Father if you cannot discipline yourself to pray. Can you imagine what your relationship would be like with your spouse or best friend if the only time you talked with him or her was in the car, at church, or just before a meal? If you're not sharing what is going on in your day with the Father God each day like you do with your special loved one, how can you expect to grow closer to Him?

Remember to save time to listen as well. This is hard and takes training. I must confess I struggle with this; as I try to empty my thoughts from my mind to hear whatever the Father might have to share, my mind tends to wonder off or I tend to doze off. It's a work in progress, and thank God He speaks to us in many other ways as well.

Here are some examples of prayers. Read them and study them; see how they spoke from their heart.

2 Chronicles 6:12–42: Solomon's prayer at the dedication of the temple.

Psalm 51:1–17: David's prayer when Nathan confronts him regarding his great sin with Bathsheba.

Jesus sums up the discipline of prayer in Matthew 6:5–14. There is the simplicity of prayer, talking with the Father God. Jesus has two things not to do: Don't pray in such a way that you bring attention to yourself. You are to bring honor to God, not yourself. Don't use empty phrases and fancy words, thinking that you will be heard for your lengthy prayers.

The Lord's Prayer simply says the following:
Greet the Father.
Give honor by recognizing Him for who He is.
Acknowledge that you wish His will to be done.
Ask for your present needs to be met.
Ask for forgiveness while you are forgiving others.
Ask for strength to overcome temptation.
Ask for deliverance from evil.

Here are some exercises. Practice them *every day*!

1) Keep it simple and personal.
2) Set prayer times.
3) Set prayer places.
4) Pray often.
5) Be attentive to the nudging of the Holy Spirit to stop and pray right then.
6) Give time to listen.

Remember, keep it simple. It's just a conversation between you and your heavenly Father. Your prayers will change as the Holy Spirit increases within you (Ephesians 6:18).

The Discipline of Obedience

You would think obedience would be easy. You would think, now that I have decided to turn my life over to God, with the help of the Holy Spirit, my new helper, obedience will be easy. You would think, but remember, Adam and Eve had only one rule to follow. How hard could that be?

We were created to make our own decisions, but since the first decision to rebel, it has been our nature not to obey. From the very beginning we have had to be trained to obey. Can you still hear your parents saying no and pushing your hand away as you reached for something you couldn't have? How long did it take for you to learn to be obedient? You will have to discipline yourself to be obedient to the Holy Spirit. Luckily, God is patient.

In Deuteronomy 28 we see that God said if we will only obey his voice and commandments, he will bless us and we will be a blessing to others. God also tells us if we do not obey his voice and commands, then we will be cursed and will be a curse to those around us. Whether our obedience to God brings about emotional or physical suffering or some type of gain, God's blessing is still a result of that obedience. With God, success is never measured by the results of the obedience, but by the act of obedience itself. You are successful when you are obedient to God. It is hard and even impossible for the world to understand that hardships brought on by obedience to God can still bring God's blessings. Obeying God always brings blessings, whether or not we get to see them or understand them (Romans 8:28).

In John 14, Jesus tells us that if we love Him, we will obey His voice, commandments, and teachings, which are recorded in His holy Word, the Bible. When we obey the laws of humanity, very rarely do we do so because of love. We obey mostly out of fear of the consequences if we do not obey. Jesus states that if we love Him, we will obey because of that love. He goes on to say that if we do not obey Him, it is because we do not have that love for Him that motivates us to do what He asks of us. As children we obey because we may fear the consequences from our parents, but as we mature we learn to obey or grant the requests of our spouse or loved ones because we love them and want to please them. Now, that doesn't mean that if we disobey sometimes, we don't love our father. From time to time for whatever reason we refuse to obey, but if we love Jesus, the Holy Spirit that came to us from our heavenly Father will not let us have peace until we address the disobedience with our Father. You must be obedient in the first thing before God will move you on to the next. If you do not obey the simplest of the Lord's commands, there are no grounds for you to obey anything. If you never learn basic math, you can never learn algebra, geometry, and physics. If you love God, you will obey God. If you obey God, you will learn to trust God.

From the very beginning, Adam, to the new heavens and earth, to eternity, it has always been and will always be about obedience. Through all that Christ accomplished in His healing, preaching, feeding the poor, teaching, and the cross, it all culminates in obedience. All in all, Jesus Christ was completely obedient to the Father God (John 6:38; 8:29; 12:49). Through your whole relationship with God the Father, what you learn, what you experience, what you share, who you are, and what you do, the bottom line is obedience!

Saul, the first king of Israel, was told once to wait for Samuel to come back and offer the sacrifice before going into battle, and then a second time he was told to totally annihilate the Amalekites, and he disobeyed God's word. He let human reasoning blur the command that God gave him, and he lost his right to the throne of Israel and God's blessing (1 Samuel 13:8–14; 15:1–23).

Be careful not to tarry when God speaks; obey immediately before human reasoning and time blur God's command.

There is a story in 1 Kings 13 about a man of God who was told by God to prophesy against King Jeroboam for the great sin of leading Israel to set up altars to worship false gods. God spoke to the man of God and told him, "Do not eat bread or drink water nor return the way by which you came." An old prophet stopped him and asked him to come home with him and eat with him. This man of God told him, "No, I cannot" and repeated to him word for word what God had told him: "You shall neither eat bread nor drink water there, nor return by the way that you came." Well, this old prophet lied to him and told him that God had spoken to him through an angel, telling him to bring the man of God back with him to eat bread and drink water at his house. The man of God believed him and did as he asked. While at the table God spoke to the old prophet, and he began to cry as he relayed the message to the man of God: "Because of your disobedience you will not be buried with your father." The man of God left the house, was met by a lion, and was attacked and killed on the road. When the old prophet heard what happened, he went to the place in the road where the man of God lay dead next to the lion that had killed him and the donkey that had carried him. The old prophet carried the body back with him and buried him in his own grave.

Thank God, disobedience is not met with lion attacks ... we would all be dead. Do you see the importance God places on obedience, though? When God tells you to do something, do it, and beware of those who may have good intentions but lead you away from obeying what you know God has told you to do.

An intimate and faithful relationship with God begins one step at a time through obedience. God will not ask you to be obedient in the big, hard things that require much trust and faith if you have not already learned trust and faith in the small, simple things through obedience to God.

God will ask you to do things that seem small, insignificant, silly, and sometimes dumb. He could tell you to take off your shoes and walk through a trail in the park while you meditate and talk to Him. He could tell you to pull into Jack in the Box halfway between Kansas and St. Louis and talk to two elderly ladies about what God is doing in your life and ask them for advice. He could tell you to grow your hair and beard long and then send you to Texas in the middle of February to camp in a tent to spend time seeking His will for your life. He could send you on a two-thousand-mile round-trip and tell you to apologize for calling your girlfriend's dad weird over the phone, not knowing they were all listening, some forty-three years later. He could even tell you to take the money he had you save; rent a ball field from the local school; rent a big tent, three hundred chairs, and two Johnny on the Spots; pull permits and inspections from the county; and have an old-fashioned tent revival for a week in July. There were no spectacular results from any of this. There were only thirty-five to forty people each night, and they were all family, friends, and church family. No one made any decisions, and it seemed as though it was unsuccessful. But it was completely successful because of obedience. Be obedient; He is training you for a closer walk with Him.

Some have walked in such an intimate relationship with God that He has asked them to do things that were just downright crazy.

Abraham, through a long walk and experience with God, and through obedience to God's commands, had acquired enough faith and trust in God to offer his son Isaac as a sacrifice without question, but with obedience to God's command to do so. It was a test of Abraham's trust in God, and God stopped Abraham's hand from harming his son. God provided the sacrifice instead (Genesis 12-22)

Here are some exercises to help you learn obedience.

1) Learn to do things you don't want to do.
2) Walk at the park on a trail or around your neighborhood barefoot, and meditate on God.
3) Walk up to people you don't know, introduce yourself, and ask them how they are. Ask if there is anything you can help them with. Ask if there is anything you can pray about for them.
4) Ask God in your walks meditating if there is something simple he would like you to do.
5) Ask Him to teach you to recognize His voice.

"We must obey God rather than men" (Acts 5:29b ESV).

"Do whatever He tells you" (John 2:5b ESV).

The Discipline of Solitude

Solitude is a state or situation in which you are alone, usually because you want to be. [24]

Solitude is an interesting word. You could be in the wilderness all alone and still not be in a state of solitude. You may well be in a situation of solitude, alone, but full of many inner concerns of loneliness, uncertainty, and inability to focus. You could as well be in a crowded room during a lecture and find yourself in a state of solitude, maybe contemplating something from earlier in the day. We might say we are "zoned out" or "daydreaming." I like what Richard Foster writes in his book *Celebration of Discipline*: "Solitude is more a state of mind and heart than it is a place" and "loneliness is inner emptiness. Solitude is inner fulfillment." [25]

If you want to experience a relationship with God to the fullest, you must discipline yourself to practice solitude.

Richard Foster in *Celebration of Discipline* goes into great detail about solitude and silence, when not to talk and when to listen. He talks as well of sporadic short moments of solitude. Again, I strongly suggest reading his book. My purpose is merely to introduce and get you started in this discipline, this training of yourself to find a place of quiet to be alone with your inner self and God ... to listen, to rest, to recharge, to meditate, to study. Solitude is the state of heart and mind necessary to receive these in the fullness of God's grace.

One only needs to look to the Bible to see how important solitude is to one's relationship with God. Two of the more prominent men in the Bible were Moses and David. Interestingly, it seems that their strong relationship with God blossomed from their time as shepherds. As they spent many lonely nights with their flocks, I am sure they found themselves in a state of solitude from time to time. I can imagine as they lay there at night looking up at the vastness of the stars on a clear night, they were in awe of their God and His creation, and wondered what God was like. I imagine they had many conversations and questions directed toward God from deep within their hearts and minds. From their many heart conversations—and dare I say even sometimes speaking the words out loud—they heard from their God, the God of their fathers. God spoke to them, God started a relationship with them, and why wouldn't He? For God promises that if we seek Him with all our heart, all our mind, and all our soul that He will hear us and we will find Him (Jeremiah 29:12–13).

In the New Testament we see Jesus withdrawing to a place of solitude and seeking solitude with His Father for guidance, encouragement, strength, rest, wisdom, reflection, and condolence.

After being baptized by John the Baptist, Jesus goes into solitude for forty days of fasting and then is tempted by satan (Matthew 4:1-11). In Luke 6:12-13, Jesus went to the mountain and prayed all night before choosing the twelve apostles who would be His closest companions. In Matthew 14:8-13, Jesus went to a desolate place by boat to be by himself after hearing of John the Baptist's death. In Matthew 14:23, Jesus, after healing and feeding a crowd of five thousand with five loaves of bread and two fish, went up to the mountain to be in solitude after He sent the disciples and crowd away. In Mark 1:35, Jesus went early in the morning while it was still dark to pray alone before leaving on a preaching tour. In Mark 6:31, Jesus told the disciples to come away by themselves to a desolate place to rest after the preaching tour they had just finished. In Luke 5:16, as the crowds grew bigger and bigger, Jesus would still withdraw to desolate places to pray. In Matthew 26:36-46, Jesus takes his closest friends to a place of solitude to pray. Jesus moves a little farther away for His solitude with His Father to talk about the painful and heart-wrenching task ahead that He was sent to accomplish.

If our example is He, how much more do we need solitude?

If you want to experience your life in Christ to the fullest, you must discipline yourself to practice solitude.

Getting started in practicing solitude is easy if you can just slow yourself down and, as they say, "Smell the roses." There is *always* time for solitude with God! *No* excuses! If you can't find time, find something to drop out of your life and make time! Even in the short moment of time it takes to stop and bend down to breathe in the fragrance of some flowers, you can have a moment of solitude with God, the great Creator, as you wonder in awe at the many beautiful flowers, each having its own soothing, pleasing fragrance. It is just amazing when you stand still in solitude in nature and contemplate all that God has created! Now, just because I gave an example of a short moment of solitude, don't think you can just cram in a bunch of short moments and continue on with your hurry-up life. We just saw several passages in which Jesus spent much time in solitude with God. It was extremely important to Jesus to spend time in solitude to get right what God's task was for Him each day.

Your times of solitude do not have to be as rigorously observed as prayer times. Your places of solitude can be many and can be the same place you go to pray. Try different places. Remember, it is more a state of the heart and mind. You could even go to a fast-food restaurant or a coffee shop, sit in the back, and ask God to show you lessons about the everyday people who are there. Listen to God, and contemplate in your heart and mind lessons of compassion, grace, forgiveness, kindness, and giving. I have a room in our basement that I use for my place of prayer, study, writing, and just spending time alone with God.

I am a maintenance supervisor at an apartment community. I perform all the maintenance requests myself, so I work alone, which allows me to take my breaks in solitude. I wonder if you caught that. I wonder if you wonder like I do. Isn't that an anomaly—being called a maintenance supervisor when you are the only one working in maintenance at that property? Who am I supposed to be supervising? Did they think I had a split personality? Is that a prerequisite for that position? Is that why there are two chairs in my shop office? Do I sit in one chair and tell myself to go do a work order and then move to the other chair and say, "No, you do it. I'm tired of doing all the work. Let me sit in the office while you go do something for a change!"? Sorry, I went off on a tangent there, but I still wonder ... which proves another point: God can use anyone, even a maintenance supervisor (even a strange one), to accomplish His will.

Here's another suggestion for training in solitude: take a trip just so you and God can be alone together. When I was a kid, my father always took us on vacations to different states each year, and he always drove so we could see the many sights along the way to our destinations. I have been privileged to see many awesome sites in this country, and we have enjoyed great family fun on those trips. I have seen Mount Rushmore, Niagara Falls, the Grand Canyon, the Rocky Mountains, the Great Smoky Mountains, Pikes Peak, the Carlsbad Caverns, Disney World, Lookout Mountain, and beaches on eastern Florida and the gulf side. As an adult I have been to the Bahamas and have driven from Kansas City to Seattle, Washington, to deliver a car to my stepdaughter. You talk about some awe-inspiring scenery that will make you wonder about creation and the God who created it ... that was a trip to inspire. I know that there is so much more in this world I could not possibly see in a lifetime, but I mention these trips to tell you that the greatest trip I ever made was to Jasper, Texas. It had nothing to do with sights or scenery. The highways through Kansas, Oklahoma, and Texas are not known for their scenery.

I had come to the point, or God had orchestrated situations in my life in such a way, that I had to find out once and for all what God wanted me to do. It was the end of January, and I prayed about it and decided to spend time alone with God camping in February. It's interesting how God works. He knew I hated the cold. Nonetheless, I picked Jasper, Texas, because the low temperatures in February were around thirty-eight and I thought I could handle that with several layers of clothes, a wool-lined sleeping bag, and a cot inside a tent. Of course, I was wrong. Did I mention I hate the cold? The first three days were miserably cold, so I moved to a screened-in pavilion covered with plastic that had electricity, and I borrowed a space heater from the pastor of Hillcrest Baptist Church, close to Martin Dies Jr. State Park where I was camping. Okay—enough complaining about the cold; I sound like the Israelis complaining during their exodus from Egypt.

Learn not to expect what you expect. To make a long story short, as they say, I did not receive the direction I went for. God has so much more in store for us than we can imagine. I shared a glorious two weeks in Bible study, walks through the pinewood trails, and watching nature in solitude with my Creator. I brought a hymnal with me and sang at night around a campfire. God directed me to Hillcrest Baptist Church. I remember sitting down in a pew near the front on Sunday morning, and the sweet spirit that I felt there brought tears to my eyes … and that was before they had started singing or the message was given. That trip was one of the most awesome experiences of my life. I might add that I looked like a homeless person, but Brother David Nugent was very gracious and kind to me. I came away from that trip with many things, but the biggest thing that God impressed on my heart was that He loved me! Because of that, no matter how down and discouraged I may find myself feeling, I am lifted up because he told me He loves me. God has no favorites; He loves you just as much as anyone! Just ask Him.

God will multiply your blessings through the discipline of solitude.

> But when He was alone with His disciples, He explained everything (Mark 4: 34b NIrV).

The Discipline of Study and Meditation

I want to discuss study and meditation together since they are practically synonymous.

> Study to shew thyself approved unto God, a workman
> that needeth not to be ashamed, rightly dividing the
> word of truth (2 Timothy 2:15 KJV).

To study is to apply oneself to the acquisition of knowledge, as by reading or investigation, to examine or investigate carefully and in detail, to think deeply, to reflect, or to consider. [26]

An accumulation of information is not knowledge. Knowledge comes from understanding, comprehending, and practicing what you study.

> My people are destroyed for lack of knowledge (Hosea
> 4:6a NASB).

So we need to practice the discipline of study. God expects us to read His Word studiously—dissecting, examining, investigating, and contemplating His every word. We must compare all things to all of God's Word, so that through the power of His Holy Spirit we might understand and comprehend the truth. Gaining this knowledge of truth is not just so we might have life more abundantly, but that we might share it with others, so that they may not be destroyed but come to the knowledge of truth as well (Ezra 7:10; Nehemiah 8:7–8, 13). It is our duty to study.

> Teach the message of truth correctly (2 Timothy 2:15b
> NIrV).

If you cannot put your thoughts into words on any subject, strive until you can. If you cannot, others will be the less fortunate and lacking all the days of their lives. Strive to reveal some truth of God's Word to yourself, and He will give that revelation to others through you. Give God the chance to pass on to others what He has shared with you. [27]

Study must be done in a place and state of solitude, for that is where your mind and heart meet to commune with God's Holy Spirit in search of the knowledge of truth.

When you study with your mind, you use intellect and reasoning. While allowing your heart to assist in your studies, you measure intellect and reasoning with all that you are—your very essence, spirit, moral values, emotions, compassion, and sympathy. This practice will cause you to think or act differently than you would with just the cold hard facts that reasoning would allow.

> The Bereans were very glad to receive Paul's message. They studied the Scriptures carefully every day. They wanted to see if what Paul said was true (Acts 17:11 NIrV).

Start your study with the Bible; determine to read it from front to back. I would suggest a good study Bible like the Life Application Study NASB. Always start your reading and studying with prayer, asking God to bless your efforts through the help of His Holy Spirit to understand and apply His Word in your life. Along with reading and studying your Bible, I would suggest a daily devotional, one that will challenge you to learn the spiritual truths of the Bible. I highly suggest *My Utmost for His Highest* by Oswald Chambers. His devotionals are so deep with spiritual truths that you could and probably should continue reading and studying them for years. It seems that each time you read it, the Spirit enlightens you with something new.

When you accepted Christ as your Savior, you were enlisted into the service of the kingdom of God. You are a defender of the kingdom, and the enemy *will* attack. The disciplines of prayer and obedience are your basic training. The discipline of study and meditation is your West Point teaching spiritual warfare tactics. The battle will start in the mind. Jesus used God's Word to win the victory over satan in His time of temptation. If we are to be victorious, we must study to understand and practice God's Word.

To meditate is to engage in contemplation or reflection, to focus one's thoughts or reflect on or ponder. [28]

To meditate is to engage in focused thought on scriptural passages or on particular doctrines or mysteries of a religion, especially Christian. [29]

Some of the synonyms for study and meditate are the same, such as consider, contemplate, ponder, and reflect. In fact, *study* is used as a synonym for meditate, and *meditate* is used as a synonym for study. [30]

With this being said, meditation in the spiritual sense is taking some word, some form of creation, some thought, some anything and considering with deep, heartfelt thought as to how it applies to God and us.

> Isaac went out to meditate in the field toward evening (Genesis 24:63a NASB).

> When I remember You on my bed, I meditate on You in the night watches (Psalm 63:6 NASB).

> I will meditate on all Your work and muse on Your deeds (Psalm 77:12 NASB).

> So I will meditate on Your wonders (Psalm 119:27b NASB).

> I meditate on all Your doings; I muse on the work of Your hands (Psalm 143:5b NASB).

> On the glorious splendor of Your majesty and on Your wonderful works, I will meditate (Psalm 145:5 NASB).

He calls me to spend time with Him in intimate thought over all the works of His hands, small or mighty.

> That I may meditate on Your word (Psalm 119:148b NASB).

> I will meditate on Your precepts (Psalm 119:15a NASB).

> Your servant meditates on Your statutes (Psalm 119:23b NASB).

> And in His law he meditates day and night (Psalm 1:2b NASB).

This book of the law shall not depart from your mouth,
but you shall meditate on it day and night, so that you
may be careful to do according to all that is written in it
(Joshua 1:8a NASB).

Meditate upon these things; give thyself wholly to them;
that thy profiting may appear to all (1 Timothy 4:15 KJV).

He calls me to meditate on His Word day and night, that I might
memorize and understand it so as to be obedient to it and that all may
profit from it.

Let the words of my mouth and the meditation of my
heart be acceptable in Your sight (Psalm 19:14a NASB).

Let my meditation be pleasing to Him (Psalm 104:34a
NASB).

The Discipline of Fasting

There seems to be a misconception that fasting is an Old Testament
thing, and it seems to be viewed by the church as having little importance
in Christian spiritual growth. That idea may have partly come from
Matthew 9:14–15, where John the Baptist's disciples came to Jesus and
asked why they and the Pharisees fasted but his disciples did not. Jesus
in turn asked how the people at a wedding could be unhappy when
the bridegroom was there. He further stated that when the bridegroom
was gone, then would be a time for fasting. I am sure that some will
disagree with me that fasting is a discipline. Fasting is a means by which
we voluntarily control the intake of what we eat or drink, for the most
part. The main purpose of fasting is not to discipline your body and
decision making, but these most surely are by-products—just as Jesus's
main purpose was not to come to Earth to set an example for us to follow,
but to offer Himself as payment for our sins for redemption unto God the
Father. His purpose was to be sacrificed; His example was a by-product.

There are different reasons why people from the Bible fasted; we will discuss those in a moment. When we fast, we are using a spiritual reason to abstain from eating or drinking for whatever period of time we decide on with God. (There are other reasons for fasting and other things that one might abstain from, but we will be talking about spiritual reasons and abstaining from food or drink.) When you purposely deprive your body of what it needs—and will most surely convince you through hunger pains you must have—you will teach, train, and discipline yourself to be obedient to God's will over what may be the will of reason. You will discipline yourself to what Jesus said in Matthew 4:4: "Man does not live by bread alone, but on every word that comes from the mouth of God." The by-product of fasting will help discipline you to put spiritual matters and God's will above your desires and the reasoning of the world.

Fasting was and is used as a means of showing just how serious the situation at hand is, and as a humbling of oneself before God as we seek His power, His mercy, and His grace in the situation before us.

After King David's great sin of adultery and the murder of Bathsheba's husband, he is told that the baby conceived during their adulterous affair would not live but would die. In 2 Samuel 12:16 we see David fasted for seven days, lying on the ground humbling himself before God, knowing how serious and grievous the situation was. He mourned and repented for his actions hoping that God might be gracious and spare the child's life.

In Jonah 3:5–9 we see the king of Nineveh and all the people hearing the warning of God's judgment against them from Jonah. Believing the situation they were in was indeed serious and grievous, they humbled themselves before God repenting from their sins, fasting and sitting in ashes, praying that God might spare them from the judgment of their evil ways.

In Nehemiah 1:1–4 after Nehemiah heard how desolate the conditions of Jerusalem and the people left behind were, he sat down, cried, mourned, and fasted for days. Hearing about the serious and grievous situation, Nehemiah confessed his sins and the nation's sins, and repented. He prayed to God to remember His promises to His people if they would turn back to Him and obey His commandments.

In chapter 4 of Esther we see another serious and grievous situation: king Ahasuerus of Susa was tricked into granting permission to all the people in the kingdom to kill the Jews and take their possessions. Queen

Esther, who was also a Jew, was asked by her uncle Mordecai to speak to the king on the Jews behalf. Queen Esther could lose her life in two ways: If she approached the king without being summoned and the king refused her, she could be put to death. And if she was granted permission to approach but did not find favor and grace in the king's eyes, then all would be lost as well. Queen Esther sent word back to her uncle asking him and all those around him to fast and pray on her behalf, as would she and all those with her.

Judges 20:26–28, Nehemiah 9, and Daniel 9:3–19 describe more situations in which God's people humbled themselves and fasted because of the seriousness of their situation.

In the first part of Matthew 4, we see Jesus fasting while in a time of temptation and instruction. We see Moses fasting as well in a time of concentrated instruction from God in Exodus 34:1–28. In Acts 13:1–3 the men of the church at Antioch fasted and prayed, laying their hands on Barnabas and Saul as they were sent out to do God's work. The spreading of the gospel of God and the calling of those sent are serious work. In times of great importance in seeking wisdom and guidance from God, one should pair fasting with prayer.

Matthew 17:14–21 tells an interesting story about a man's son who was possessed by demons; the disciples could not cast out the demons. When Jesus was told that his disciples could not heal him, he rebuked them as an unbelieving and perverted generation. In private He told the disciples it was because of their lack of faith, and he said besides, "Howbeit this kind goeth not out but by prayer and fasting (Matthew 17:21 KJV)." It would seem that true fasting has some God-given power to it. And what is the kind of true fasting that God will accept? In Isaiah 58 we see that a true fast is not the show of it—the bowing down to the ground, the spreading of ashes and wearing sackcloth, and a show of us being humble and repentant. God said He's not buying it; He can see straight to the heart of it. God said, how can you make a sacrifice to me through fasting when you refuse to sacrifice to those around you in need? How can you come before Me pretending you are giving up food for me when you do not give up food for the hungry? How can you come to Me asking my help through your fast and yet you give no help to the helpless and hopeless?

In Matthew 6:16–18, Jesus teaches about true and false fasting. He tells us that those hypocrites who look gloomy, sad, and mopey so that everyone knows they are fasting have their reward in the false sense of honor they believe they receive from others noticing their fast. Jesus tells us if we are serious in fasting the true way, toward God, then we should wash our face and be well groomed. "So that your fasting will not be noticed by men, but by your Father who is in secret, and your Father who sees what is done in secret will reward you" (Matthew 6:18).

Prayer is powerful in seeking God's will and intercession in our situation and in those of others. Some situations may seem so serious and grievous that we feel helpless even though we come before God in prayer. As we saw above, some things need the added power of fasting. With fasting we need to evaluate ourselves before we come to God with our request. We need to search ourselves, confess our sins before God, and repent of them. We need to humble ourselves realizing that God is all-powerful, He is the one that sustains our life, and we can do nothing without Him. Know as well that even though we pray and fast in the way that honors God, He is not obligated to give us what we ask. Remember that even though King David prayed and fasted for seven days in humility and repenting of sins, God did not honor his request. God honors our sincere prayers and fasting, but He will answer in His will, having our best interest in mind. God may not bless in the way we were expecting, but He still blesses sincere prayers and fasts.

It would be wise if you feel the desire to fast to consider your health. If you have health issues, you should consult your physician. Consult with God through prayer and meditation about the duration of your fast, what you will be abstaining from, and the situation that has led to your desire to fast before God. Be sincere, humble, and repentant. Remember this is between God and you. You can't fake it; God sees into your heart. Look for God to bless you as only He can as you honor Him in fasting and prayer.

In my younger days I had fasted for one day, two days, and three days. My fast would be drinking only water, sometimes only milk shakes, and sometimes nothing—neither food nor drink. I fasted over some very serious situations in my life that involved not only me but others … and we know we can't change what other people do. God does not change people against their will, but He will give many opportunities for change. Although the outcomes of my fasts and prayers were not always what I was looking for, I always felt blessed afterward. I knew that God was changing me, giving peace in the situation, and acknowledging my concerns.

I wish I could say that I was always close to God, desiring to be obedient, but that's not the case. I felt that God was calling me into the ministry, but my marriage did not support that, and I became confused and angry with God. I had enough of trying to make sense of what I felt God wanted me to do and the situation I was in. I gave up and ran from God for some fifteen years. My mother always tried to convince me to get back to church, even after her death. A mother's prayers are strong.

I mentioned earlier that I went to Jasper, Texas, to find out what God wanted me to do with my life. I was so frustrated with my life that I thought if I would just go somewhere in solitude and fast for forty days and nights, God would surely let me know what he wanted me to do with my life. I know ... what a harebrained idea! So there I stood in front of a counter, my charge card in hand ready to pay for six weeks of camping. The clerk behind the counter said they could take payment for only two weeks—they were going to change over to a new computer system in two weeks, and the payment would not transfer over. She said that after the two weeks I could come back and then pay for the other four weeks. God is good. He knew that even as hardheaded and slow as I am, He didn't need more than two weeks to teach me what I needed to know.

My tent was set up, and I was all set to begin my fast and have time alone with God. I have to say, the first three days were some of the most miserable days physically in my life. It was cold, it rained the whole time, and it was so windy I thought my tent might blow down. On the end of the third day of my fast I could not sleep for more than an hour at a time. I had one of the worst headaches that I could remember in a long time, I could not get warm, and I shivered all night long. It would take me one hour to fall asleep just to wake up in an hour from the pain and shivering and then to spend another hour trying to get back to sleep. This went on for ten hours, from eight at night till around six in the morning. At around six in the morning I was awakened by an audible whisper in my left ear, "I love you, Jerry." Believe what you wish here, but I know what I believe. If you are sincere in your efforts to find God, He will reveal Himself to you.

I was able to fast for only three days, but God honored my sincere effort by revealing that He loves me and telling me to trust that He is in control. I did not get my answers to what His plans were for me, but I came away knowing what He wanted me to do. He wants me to love Him as He loves me. He wants me to love others as He loves me. He wants me to have a relationship with Him daily, just like I have relationships with other people, on a day-by-day basis. He wants me to trust that when He wants me to do something special for Him, He will let me know. Until then I am to live life as Jesus did, showing compassion for all and telling the good news where and whenever the opportunity arises. One day at a time. One step at a time.

Chapter 9

Personal Disciplines: One-on-One with the Lord and Directed Outward

The Discipline of Humility

> Humble: not proud or arrogant; to lower in condition, importance, or dignity. [31]
>
> To know your place before God and humanity in a biblically healthy and realistic way (my definition).

Origin of Humble

> From Old French—From Latin—*humus,* ground—*humilis,* low, lowly [32]
>
> From Old French—From Latin—*humus,* earth—*humilis,* "literally" on the ground [33]

Root Words Hum *and* Humanus

These root words are *Hum* and *Humanus*, which come from the Latin *humus*, meaning Earth and ground, and the Latin *humanus*, which means man. It is interesting to follow the changes in idea here. It begins with *HUMus*, earth, then becomes *HUMble*, lowly; and finally to *HUMAN*, man. But we must never forget the origin of humanity: "Dust thou art and to dust thou must return" (Genesis 3:19). [34]

Being humble is being human.

It is interesting, the display of anguish that God's people showed by tearing their clothes and throwing dust on their heads and/or lying on the ground. Joshua tore his clothes, fell to the ground, and threw dust on his head after the defeat at Ai (Joshua 7:6). Many of the Jews cast dust on their heads over the destruction of Jerusalem (Lamentations 2:10) as well over the destruction of Tyre (Ezekiel 27:30). It is a powerful display of the fact that "naked I came into this world and naked I shall return!" and "to the ground you return, for out of it you were taken, for dust you are and to dust you shall return" (my paraphrase of Job 1:21 and Genesis 3:19).

It would be helpful to go back and reread chapter three: "The need to be humble."

Pride, the opposite of humility, is the original sin in thought that allowed the original sin in action: rebellion. Satan could not humble himself, but he wanted to be like God and rebelled against God. Satan tempted Eve and Adam with pride. They could not humble themselves when satan told them they could be like God if they ate the fruit of the Tree of Knowledge of Good and Evil and rebelled against God.

> "Blessed are those who are free of pride. They will be given the earth" (Matthew 5: 5 NIrV).

Vanity, stubbornness, and exclusion are blocks to humility.

In Deuteronomy 8:2–3, 16 God led the Israelites through the wilderness for forty years, hungry and thirsty, to teach them humility. God was the one that fed them and gave them water to drink when there was none to be found. God delivered them from their enemies in miraculous ways, that they would not boast of their own accomplishments, but would humble themselves before God and know that He is in control.

In James 4:6 we see that "God opposes the proud, but gives grace to the humble." In 1 Peter 5: 5–6, we are instructed to put on humility toward one another as though it was our clothing. In Job 2:12 we see a great example of this when Job's friends tore their clothes, threw dust on their heads, sat on the ground next to him, and said nothing for seven days. By doing so they clothed themselves with humility and shared in their friend's suffering. We are to have compassion, not the kind that merely feels sorry for others, but the kind that suffers with them in their pain and anguish.

Paul, in 2 Corinthians 12:20–21, speaks of situations where God may humble us that we might be brokenhearted over the sins of our brothers in Christ and pray that they might be convicted by the Holy Spirit and repent of their sins

> You are God's chosen people. You are holy and dearly loved. So put on tender mercy and kindness as if they were your clothes. Don't be proud. Be gentle and patient. Put up with each other. Forgive the things you are holding against one another. Forgive, just as the Lord forgave you. And over all of those good things put on love. Love holds them all together perfectly as if they were one (Colossians 3:12–14 NIrV).

We are to humble ourselves under the mighty hand of God. So then if we wish to grow in our relationship with God the Father, we must learn and train ourselves to be humble before God and humanity.

Pharaoh would not humble himself and suffered greatly at the hand of God through all the plagues sent throughout Egypt, eventually taking the life of his son (Exodus 7–12). King Nebuchadnezzar did not humble himself and spent seven years in the fields eating grass like cattle, and becoming hairy with nails that grew like birds' claws (Daniel 4:28–37).

Jesus said in Matthew 23:12, "Whoever exalts himself will be humbled."

2 Chronicles 7:14 tells us that if we will humble ourselves and pray, God will hear us, forgive us, and heal our brokenness. In 2 Chronicles 34:27–28, because King Josiah humbled himself before God, God told him that he heard him, that he would die with his fathers before him in peace, and that He would spare him from the destruction to come. Ahab, a very evil king, because he humbled himself before God, was told that the evil promised him would be delayed to his next generation (1 Kings 21:27–29).

It is obvious that we are here today and gone tomorrow. In Luke 12: 16–20, the rich man with more crops than space to store them tore down his barns and built larger barns to hold it all. In his pride he told himself,

"I have all I need for many years," and he told himself to relax and be merry for all he had accomplished. God told him, "Fool, tonight your soul is required of you and none of that matters." We are in control of nothing. What we have is God's. He is in control.

Humble yourself, or you will be humbled (my paraphrase of Matthew 23: 12).

Affliction will humble you, whether it be physical or emotional. It will cut to the very core of your heart; it will pierce you through. That moment when it stings you, you realize you are no different than anyone else. You were born of this Earth, and to this Earth you will return … as a fading flower in its beauty today, scorched by the sun, and blown away tomorrow. Be thankful for affliction, and let it have its way to humble and teach you.

If you are being afflicted, check to see if God is trying to use it to humble you, to teach you something.

> Think of yourselves the way Christ Jesus thought of himself. He had equal status with God but didn't think so much of himself that he had to cling to the advantages of that status no matter what. Not at all. When the time came, he set aside the privileges of deity and took on the status of a slave, became human! Having become human, he stayed human. It was an incredibly humbling process. He didn't claim special privileges. Instead, he lived a selfless, obedient life and then died a selfless, obedient death—and the worst kind of death at that—a crucifixion (Philippians 2: 5–8 MSG).

God has told us; do what is right, love kindness, and *walk humbly* before God (my paraphrase of Micah 6:8).

The Discipline of Patience

In our culture I wonder if there is anything more difficult to practice than patience. As I mentioned before, I work in apartment maintenance, and troubleshooting air conditioners during the summer months will sometimes try my patience, for mostly one reason. The thermostats that we use have a five-minute delay before turning on the AC unit after the thermostat calls for cooling. I know that, I know that, I know that, but when you have a poor concept of how long five minutes should be, it tends to seem like ten minutes. So there I stand waiting for it to come on, and when it seems to take too long, the wheels start turning in my head. I start going through all kinds of scenarios of why it's not coming on, other than the fact that I'm just impatient. We are all in a hurry to get somewhere. Hurry is a disease that will deprive you of life.

Think about this if you will. The Bible says to "Wait upon the Lord" and that "a day is like a thousand years unto the Lord" (Proverbs 20:22, 2 Peter 3:8). God is outside of time; in His realm time means nothing. With that concept of time, if God thought about not answering me for a day, I would have been dead about nine hundred years before his answer arrived. His Word also says that God is not slow to make good his promises in our concept of time, but that he is patient toward us. He is faithful and knows the right time to answer. So patience becomes a matter of trust.

The next time you are waiting on God and it seems like the answer is not coming, have patience. Have trust in God. Know that He controls the delay. The reason for the delay on the thermostat is to protect the heart of the AC system, which is the compressor. The delay gives time for the pressures to balance out in the systems to protect the compressor from unnecessarily high pressure at start-up. God uses delay in the same way. He is protecting you from unnecessary pressure and will balance out the right conditions at the right time so that your life might produce what it was created for.

Of course, sometimes the AC never comes on, and then I need to find out what is broken. The same thing holds true when we are not hearing from God—we need to know where the relationship with our heavenly Father broke down. Find it, fix it, have patience, and trust God.

Okay, so we all know that we need patience. If we want a closer relationship with the Father, then we need to be more like Jesus. If we don't have patience, then how can we show love and compassion to those who try our patience? And if we don't show love and compassion, then how are we any different from anyone else? As a matter of fact, some people who are not Christians do show love and compassion. Our lack of such will drive people away from Christ, not to Christ. So what can we do to train ourselves and learn patience?

Go back and learn to be humble! We are no better than anyone else. We want people to have patience with us, so we should treat others as we wish to be treated. Again, slow down and get the hurry out of you. Think before you react. There are always things going on in other people's lives that we know nothing about. They, just like we, need love and compassion, and God's Word says that if we love Him, then we will show love and compassion to others.

Before I worked for Coca-Cola as a field service tech (yes, I've had many different jobs—a jack-of-all-trades and a master of none), I would get angry and impatient with drivers on the road. Why can't you use your turn signal? Do you need a forty-acre field to go? I would like to at least do the speed limit here; move or get off. One of my favorites was, "Where did you get your license, at an amusement park?" When I had no idea where I was going, I would drive slowly looking for a street, and I would change lanes in a hurry when I realized that my destination was on the other side of the road. It made me realize that other people might not know where they were going, that there just might be a good reason for the way they were driving. And, of course, I got paid whether I was driving or working on some machine ... so what was the hurry? The patience I learned from that carried over to my own travels. Of course, I still mumble under my breath from time to time, but we are all a work in progress.

A lack of patience causes a lot of stress. Here are just a few things you can purposely do to increase patience and lower you stress level (eventually):

- Go to the longest line at the cash register even if you have only one or two items.
- When you see someone with twenty-five items in the twenty or less lane, let them go in front of you. When you are stuck in traffic, let people in line instead of riding someone's bumper to keep others from butting in front of you.
- If you are running late, let it go. Don't try to make up the time by hurrying; as a matter of fact, pull off the road and thank God for a wonderful day.

- Don't make excuses for being impatient, but apologize for your actions to the recipient of your impatience.
- Put yourself in situations that make you impatient with the forethought of overcoming and making it a blessing to someone, even if you are the only one blessed by it.

Humility will help you become patient, and patience will help you become humble.

The Discipline of Simplicity

It's funny—right away I worry about not having enough to say about being simple. We always want to make things more difficult than they need to be. We make life difficult. It was meant to be simple and started out simple in the garden of Eden. All they had to do was take care of the garden, and enjoy one another and their relationship with God. Our culture is a far cry from that!

Do you want to know how to discipline yourself to be simple? It's simple! Jesus said become a child.

Read Matthew 18:1–6. The disciples had just been arguing about who was the greatest among them. I am sure they were all measuring their accomplishments against those of the others, or their importance to the group. Judas Iscariot might have said, "Obviously I am, since I am in charge of the money." A couple of them might have thought they were greater, because Jesus spent more time with them, or maybe because they were not afraid to speak and seemed to have all the right answers. Maybe the argument started because Jesus took only Peter, James, and John up on the mountain where Jesus was transfigured into his glorious body. Nonetheless, Jesus perceived what they were arguing about and inquired about their discussion, and afraid to admit it, they kept quiet. Once they were in the house they asked Him, "Who is the greatest in the kingdom of Heaven?" His answers were simple: unless you convert and become as a little child, you can't even enter the kingdom, and whoever humbles himself as a little child will be greatest in the kingdom.

I like how "The Message" Bible reads in this passage of Matthew 18. The subheading for this passage is "Whoever becomes simple again." In the passage it says whoever becomes "simple and elemental" like a child will be greatest in the kingdom. I don't know about you, but I don't want to be the greatest in the kingdom, but I do want to be there. I want a closer walk with God until I get there, and Jesus says it's not going to happen unless I become like a simple little child.

So what does it mean to be simple like a child? I will share my take on it, and I'm sure you can sit down in a quiet place and arrive at your understanding of what that looks like. Of course, we are talking about a little child who has not been tainted by the adult world. First, a little boy worries for nothing; his father takes care of his needs (like our heavenly Father promises us). His job is enjoying life the way it was meant to be, like in the garden. He takes it one day at a time; he is never in a hurry (especially when he is called by a parent). He enjoys the people around him and does not judge. He is caring and loving. He forgives easily and does not hold grudges. He wishes to please his parents.

Look at your complicated, hurry-up life. How can you make it simple?

The Discipline of Submission

No one likes to be told what to do, especially if we don't agree with it! To submit is not something that we usually do willingly. It is to yield to some higher rank or authority. Surrender is one of the synonyms for submit. The picture of surrender in war is that you have come to a rationalization that the power before you controls your situation, and the best response is to yield, surrender, and/or submit to that power. So when God's Word tells us to submit, He is not asking us necessarily to like it, agree with it, or understand it, but to do it.

In Genesis 16, Hagar was Sarai's maid; Sarai sent Hagar into Abram that he might have a child with her, since Sarai could not conceive. When Sarai saw that Hagar was pregnant, she regretted her decision and mistreated her to the point that Hagar ran away. The angel of the Lord told her to return to her mistress, Sarai, and to submit herself to her authority. The Hebrew word *anah* used in this passage is a verb meaning to be bowed down, occupied, or afflicted. [35] Hagar was told to subject herself to Sarai's rule over her. The angel did not say Sarai would be kind to her, but that it was her duty to obey whether or not she agreed with her. That is what God is saying to us when He says we are to submit to authority, those who rank higher than we, all the way up to God. Like it or not, the wife is to be subject to the husband, and the husband to the church. He never said the authorities over us had to be fair; that's part of the definition of submit. It's a duty that doesn't need our approval.

We are told that we are to submit to our leaders (Hebrews 13:17), to God (James 4:7), to civil authorities (1 Peter 2:13), and to our elders (1 Peter 5:5).

I'm not going to speak about submitting to God, because I believe that subject is a given. We usually don't have a problem submitting to God, because we respect Him and trust Him to do what is right. It is the humans that we don't respect and trust.

1 Peter 5 says to submit to those who are older and to submit to one another. We are to respect our elders and yield to the wisdom they have gained. Likewise, we should respect and yield to one another so that we may love one another, and not fight and bicker.

1 Peter 2 talks about submitting to our civil authorities, which would be our elected officials from the president on down to the police. The way we respect them and obey them is a reflection on God, for it is His will that we do so. Again, I feel the need to repeat that our submission has nothing to do with whether we agree with them, or whether or not they treat us with respect. Yes, there are officials and police who abuse their authority, but is our duty to God to obey and respect. Peter goes on to say there is no virtue in accepting punishment that you deserve, but when you are mistreated for doing good and continue to do good despite the unjust treatment, then you are honoring God, and that's what matters.

Jesus said, "Give to Caesar what is Caesar's, but give to God what is God's" (Matthew 22:21). There will come a day, even in America, when you will have to make a decision whether to obey God or humans. One-day government will outlaw the Gospel of Jesus; on that day you will have to decide whom you will obey. John and Peter stood before the Jewish authorities when they were told to stop preaching the gospel and stated, "Whether it is right in God's sight to obey man rather than God, you be the judge, but we cannot stop preaching what we have seen" (Acts 4:19). Later, Peter and the other apostles were thrown into prison for preaching again. An angel of the Lord came and let them out of prison and told them to go back to the temple and preach again. The authorities found them there preaching, brought them back, and questioned them saying, "Did we not command you not to preach again?" Peter and the other apostles answered, "We must obey God rather than men!" (Acts 5:29)

Hebrews 13 talks about our submission to our spiritual leader. This is God's Word; we have to take it as coming from the authority of God. All Scripture is from the authority of God. You cannot pick and choose whom you submit to if you love God. It is stated here that we must put ourselves under the authority and obey our leaders. They know they are accountable to God, and they watch over the flock that God has put them over. We are to obey them so that their work will be a joy to them. If we quarrel, bicker, complain, and try to tell them how to do the job that God has placed them in, it won't do any of us any good. Too many of God's churches suffer and sometimes fall apart because we don't love God enough to submit to the God-given authority of our spiritual leaders.

How do you learn to submit? Simple!

You obey God's Word and just do it!

The Discipline of Service

What is our service?

If you look up the definition of service, you will see something like this: The providing or a provider of accommodations and activities required by the public, as maintenance service, TV repair service, telephone service, bus service, water service, electric service, and on and on.

Just this morning I was checking Facebook, and there was the description of our service. (I didn't know that God was on Facebook.) A Facebook friend shared a TBN video of Pastor J. John describing his occupation. He said if we are followers of Jesus, then we all work for a global enterprise that has networks in almost every country. We have hospitals, hospice, homeless shelters, marriage work, orphanages, feeding programs, and educational work. We deal in the area of behavioral alterations. Basically, we look after people from birth to death. That enterprise is called the church! [36]

Our service is to provide hope—physically, mentally, emotionally, and more importantly, spiritually—just as Jesus did.

When we think of service for the Lord, we tend to make it more than what it really is for most of us. We think about the service of pastor, youth pastor, music leader, deacon, nursery worker, the church committees, missionaries, evangelists, and Bible study leaders, but it is more simple than that. (There's that word again: *simple*.)

Our service is to be a Christian, Christ like. Every day and every moment it is our service to do what Christ did. We are to love with that unconditional love and show kindness every moment of our lives, whether we feel like it or not, whether people deserve it or not. We are to show compassion whether it falls on ungrateful people or not. We are to help the poor and needy in secret so that our reward comes from God and not the show of it before humanity. We are not to judge but to show compassion. Jesus chose to show compassion, not judgment, and we should as well. It is our service to show Jesus in all we do, every moment of our lives, and to treat others the way we wish to be treated. It is our service to share the gospel, the good news of Jesus at every opportunity given us.

I once planned a vacation to go away and write. I was going to spend two nights in Kansas City with a friend and visit step kids (although they are adults, can you say step-adults?), and then stay in Abilene, Kansas. I had planned to leave at 4:00 p.m. so I could arrive at my friend's at a decent time. Well, a hot-water tank leaked and needed to be replaced, and I didn't have one or a way to get one. Great—there went my plans. Well, the problem was solved with twenty minutes to spare. Then I got a call from someone who needed help with an AC that was frozen, and they were selling the house. I explained that I was leaving for vacation and was finishing up a hot-water tank installation and wouldn't be able to help. He continued to ask who else might be able to do the work. I suggested someone and asked where the man's home was. It turned out it was on my way to Kansas City, so I agreed to look at it. I fretted from the moment I realized the tank needed to be replaced all the way to finishing the AC job. I worried for nothing. A wrench was thrown into my plans, and it upset me. Why? It doesn't even bother me now. As a matter of fact, as I left the AC job I was feeling good that I had helped someone. Of course, I arrived two hours later than I had wanted to, but my friend was okay with that.

All this is to say, we make life more difficult than it is. Our plans should not stop us from being of service to others. Yes, it could have been that my car was full of kids who were all hungry, crabbing for food, and then I would have had to say no. It was just me, though. So if we can change our plans to help, that is part of our service. It wasn't a service that someone was saved; it was just a service that showed the everyday opportunities to care and help. Our service is not about us but is about everyone else.

Our service is to live the attributes of Jesus every day and every moment.

How do we do that?

Pray every morning that God, through the power of His Holy Spirit, makes you more like Jesus in your heart and mind, that He opens your eyes to the opportunities for service each day and gives you the strength to obey.

Chapter 10

Personal Disciplines in Various Group Settings

The Discipline of Worship

What is worship?

The many Hebrew and Greek words that were used to translate the word *worship* had these definitions: to bow down, to do homage, to do obeisance, to kiss the ground before a superior, I reverence, I adore, I serve, to show piety toward. [37]

After researching several definitions, my definition of worship would be as follows: to give deep respect with awe, acknowledging the overwhelming worthiness of God.

The Bible is full of different ways of worshiping God. David and the early Jews were very expressive in their worship. They danced in the streets and made melodies with all kinds of instruments. They praised God in song, giving glory in the many wonders done for them, rejoicing and shouting praises for His great mercies. David was so expressive in his dancing for joy as they brought in the Ark of the Covenant, that his wife told him he made a fool of himself in front of all the women servants.

Somewhere along the line, worship was contained in a temple. Then along came Jesus to talk about true worship.

The woman at the well said to Jesus, "Our fathers used to worship in this mountain, and your people say Jerusalem is the place where people are supposed to worship." Jesus told her there is a time when you will not worship here or in Jerusalem, and the time is now. He went on to say true worshippers will worship the Father in spirit and truth, for those are the people that the Father seeks to be His worshippers. Jesus told her that the Father is Spirit, and people who wish to worship Him must do so in spirit and truth (John 4: 7–24).

So, yes, you can worship God in the woods or in a boat on the lake. I've been there, done that. I worshipped for about two minutes and fished for about two hours, so I'm just not buying it. I highly doubt you are sincere when you say you can worship God in the woods or the water just as well as in a church.

There are times of individual worship in the Bible, but I think they were really more times of solitude where worship was a part of that time alone with God. For the most part, worship was done in masses of people as in the stories of David, Solomon, Ezra, Nehemiah, and others. Maybe the greatest time of worship was on the day of Pentecost, when they were all gathered together, the Holy Spirit descended on them, and they spoke in many different languages. The people were amazed and in awe, praising God for the many wonders done by the apostles. Hebrews 10:25 tell us to not forsake the assembling as some do, but to come together to encourage and share with one another.

As I have mentioned, I went to Hillcrest Baptist Church in Jasper, Texas, and I noted how sweet the spirit was there. I believe there were people there that prepared their spirits for worship, or the sweet spirit that I felt would not have been there. Jesus said that God is Spirit and we must worship in spirit. My spirit worships with God's Spirit. We must prepare our spirits for worship. Sometime before the service go to God and ask Him to fill your spirit with the awe and overwhelming presence of His great love and grace, that it might overflow into other people's spirits as well, creating such a sweet unity of spirit that no one will go untouched by His Word … that we will let the spirit move so we might worship Him in songs of praise to the top of our lungs and shout amen to His Word.

The Discipline of Fellowship

The Hebrew and Greek words used to translate the word fellowship have definitions as follows: be joined, unite, contributory help, sharing in fellowship in spirit, sharing, people sharing something held in common, I am a partaker with. [38]

I will concede that the word *fellowship* as used in the Bible does not have the same meaning as we use today in our churches. It displays more the idea of sharing as a group in the same spirit, sharing in the lives of fellow believers whether that be spiritual or physical, rejoicing with or suffering with, encouraging and counseling one another. I believe the idea of fellowship used in our churches are to be displayed in the context 0f Acts 2 and 4. The early Christians were a very close group during that period. They sold all that they had, gave to the church, lived with the church, ate with the church, and shared their lives with each other. Living together like that is the essence of biblical fellowship.

In my opinion, all of our churches are failing at this discipline of fellowship. Are we all too big and busy to realize the damage of not having fellowship as a body of believers in Christ? Do we not see the advantage of sharing our lives with each other, the personal things that can't be shared in a worship service? Fellowship is the means we need to find new friends who can encourage us and help us grow spiritually. Fellowship gives us the opportunity to welcome in the new Christians, show them love and support, get to know them and let them know us, and help them feel like part of the family. Fellowship allows even those who are longtime members to enjoy like-minded friends in Christ.

What do we need to do?

We need to talk to the leaders of our churches and persuade them to take action in bringing this discipline back to our churches.

I'm just as guilty as the next person on this subject. I don't think that small groups in your church are serving the same purpose as fellowship. Small groups usually run in increments of weeks and are usually discussing some book or following a particular curriculum. If a new member wants to join in midstream it is confusing. Fellowship is not a structured meeting with an itinerary other than getting to know one another and enjoying one another's presence. I don't have all the answers, but once or twice a year does not cut it either. If you can't persuade the leaders of the importance of fellowship, take the mission on yourself.

The Discipline of Confession

From my study of the Hebrew words translated as *confess*, the idea in the Old Testament of confessing your sins was the picture of your sins being "cast" off from you onto a live goat and sent away into the wilderness carrying your sins away. Another goat was used as a blood sacrifice to God to atone for sin (Leviticus 16: 1-22). [39]

Now the New Testament came when Christ died on the cross, taking all of our sins with Him. He did not stay in the grave with them, but raised from the grave alive carrying them with Him to the Father once and for all and in essence saying, "I have accepted all their debt, given my life in exchange, raised from the grave and carried their sins away."

One of the Greek words used to translate confess gives the idea of "acknowledging" sin. [40] Since Christ's death and resurrection, when we confess our sins, we acknowledge them before Christ. In essence we say, "Jesus, I know I messed up again. I know what I did was wrong, I know you have forgiven me, and I know I need to not do it again. Jesus, I need your help to do right." My sins are already forgiven, but each time I must acknowledge what I did, what it cost me and others, and most of all what it cost Jesus to have already forgiven me.

James 5:16 says to confess your faults one to another … It is interesting how that reads when you use the definitions of the Greek word translated "confess." The definitions are as follows: I consent fully, I agree out and out, I confess, I admit, I acknowledge. [41] The archaic or old definition of consent is to agree in sentiment, and sentiment is a feeling or emotion. With that said, I wish to paraphrase James 5:16 as such: "Acknowledge, fully admit, and fully agree with feeling and emotion your faults one to another, and pray for one another, that you might be healed. For the effectual, compassionate, spirit-filled prayer of a righteous man brings much advantage."

I don't believe that this is saying we need to confess all our sins to one another, but there are sins we need help to overcome. We don't confess with others for forgiveness unless they are the ones we sinned against in some way, but we go to them for godly advice and prayer. We need someone whom we can have complete confidence in, someone whom we can trust to keep our confessions and conversations confidential. We need to be fully honest and sincere with the person we come to, and that person needs to be godly, honest, sincere, compassionate, and trustworthy. Your conversations should always be showered in prayer.

Pray that God will make you aware of your sins, that you might acknowledge them before Him. Thank Him for forgiving you, and ask Him to help you keep from sinning again. If you have a sin that you cannot remove from your life, or one that lies heavy on your heart, seek a trustworthy person who can spiritually help with your situation. Remember, shower it all with prayer.

The Discipline of Guidance

Humble in the Spirit be guided, mature in the Spirit lead, in the unity of one Spirit. There are two classifications of guidance that we need to address: individual guidance and corporate guidance. Both need to be led by the Holy Spirit.

John 14:16–17, 26 Jesus tells us the Father will give us a Helper and He will be with us forever. He is the Spirit of truth, and we will know Him because He lives in us. The Helper, the Holy Spirit, sent by the Father will teach all things and bring to our memory all that he has told us. In John 16:13 we are told that when He, the Spirit of truth comes, He will guide us in all truth. Whatever He hears from the Father He will speak to us.

If we are going to live a life that reflects Jesus and honors God, then we need a guide; that guide is God's Word and the Holy Spirit. We need to continually spend time reading and studying God's Word so that we know the right direction to take. If we do not know His Word, then how can the Holy Spirit bring it to our memory?

We need to practice listening for the voice and nudging of the Holy Spirit. I am not sure if I can explain completely how to do that. This should go without saying, but I will say it again: you have to have confessed Jesus as your Savior in order for the Holy Spirit to be in you guiding you. The Holy Spirit speaks to nonbelievers for only one purpose, to convict them of their need for salvation. Once you are saved, He is there as your helper and guide.

If you are a new Christian, you may remember the voice in your mind that was telling you your need to be saved. Maybe the voice was telling you to step out and go forward to the front and tell the pastor that you wish to be saved, or maybe the voice was nagging at you to ask someone what you needed to do to be saved. I'll bet you kept arguing with it. You kept telling it not now, later. You probably tried to rationalize with it. You may have kept ignoring it until the voice finally gave up on you. I am not saying that is the only way He speaks to us, but I tend to think it may be the most common way. God is God and cannot be held down to one way of speaking. Some in the Bible were fortunate enough to hear Him audibly. When you are seeking an answer from God on some particular question, He might use a particular Scripture to speak to you, maybe through some person. It could even be a particular phrase in a movie, but you need to be conditioned to know it is from God.

I have already mentioned that you need to be reading and studying God's Word so you have a guide and knowledge to be sure that what you believe to be the Spirit talking to you is in line with God's Word. The Holy Spirit will *never* tell you anything that contradicts God's Word. You need to establish a prayer relationship with God. You need to be obedient to God's Holy Spirit. Paul said in 1 Thessalonians 5:19, Do not put the Holy Spirit out (my paraphrase). If you know God wants you to do something and you don't do it, that is putting the Holy Spirit out. It's like pouring water on a fire—the more you disobey, the more water you pour on the Holy Spirit. Unlike fire, though, you can never completely put out the Holy Spirit, because God put it there as a seal of His promise when you accepted Christ as your Savior. You can, however, through disobedience smother it to the point that it is unrecognizable to anyone but God. It is always there and can be fanned to fullness by obedience to God at any time. It is my belief that you need these basic disciplines to recognize the prompting of the Holy Spirit as He guides you. When you hear and obey God's guidance, you will have peace and comfort within your spirit. Obey the guidance of the Holy Spirit.

Corporate guidance would work if all the individuals were guided by the Holy Spirit. In the early church mentioned in Acts 2 and 4, there were well over three thousand people, and the Scriptures said they were of one mind, heart, and soul. How that many people, much less church members, were of one mind, heart, and soul is a miracle in and of itself. They were, of course, new Christians open to the leadership of the newly acquired Holy Spirit, and their leaders were filled with the Spirit. Time and pride have a way of hardening our hearts to the unifying efforts of the Holy Spirit.

This body of believers that proclaim Jesus Christ as their Savior for the debt of sin that humanity could not pay, but only Him, are corporately unified in Spirit to at least this one truth: "There is no other way to the Father, but through His Son Jesus Christ!"

In churches it is difficult to make corporate decisions about many operations. Always the guidance of the Holy Spirit needs to be consulted. The decisions need to be made in the unity of the Holy Spirit, not by a simple majority. Too many times decisions are made by calculating numbers, seeking professional help, and rationalization, with very little thought to what the Spirit has to say. Of course, those things need to be taken into consideration, but they neither make nor break a decision made by the unity of the Spirit. I believe any idea or proposal needs to be showered with prayer just to see if it is worthy of the Spirit. Then bring it to the people and ask them to pray about it and see if there is a unity of Spirit among the people to proceed. Let the Holy Spirit guide the people by unifying their spirits on these decisions. This does not mean all will agree, but keep praying about it as a body of believers until those who don't agree can at least come to a peace that they may not understand and agree, but they have been put at peace by the Holy Spirit about it. If a unity of Spirit cannot be reached, then I believe it should be dropped until such unity can be reached at some later time as led by the Spirit. Unity of the Spirit in the people is more important than a simple or three-fourths majority.

I am not a pastor, so I cannot speak from that experience, but I am a layperson who has been part of decisions in which there was no unity of Spirit in the choices made by the churches I have been members of. Some of those decisions resulted in total dispersion of the church and some with people leaving mad and hurt. Always, always everything needs to be showered and covered with prayer, love, compassion, and forgiveness. Seek reconciliation if possible.

The Discipline of Celebration

As I sit here writing, I can't get that song out of my head— "Celebrate good times, come on!" For one year, or maybe even to this day, the St. Louis Cardinals played this over and over, so now it is embedded in everybody's head in St. Louis. I'm not much of a baseball fan (which is probably odd for my having lived in St. Louis all my life), so I don't know if they still play it. Seriously, if anyone has something to celebrate, it should be Christians! We have hope! We have it here and in the afterlife—no more tears, no more sorrows, and no more pain!

We all get down, and we all get depressed from time to time, but we need to seriously tell ourselves tomorrow is a better day. I may be upset because my feet get wet because my shoes have a hole, but at least I'm not barefoot. I might complain about under- or overcooked food, but at least I have food. We hear it over and over again, but don't make yourselves cold to the fact that there is always someone better off and always someone worse off than you are. Paul of the Bible learned how to be content when he was hungry and when he was full. He learned to live with little or much. He learned to be content in whatever his situation. Paul suffered many things— he was beaten, thrown in jail, stoned and left for dead—but Paul learned the secret of doing all things through Christ who strengthened him. Jesus is our joy and our celebration. If we can focus on Him, then life is a celebration.

We need to quit living our lives with frowns on our faces, short tempers, hurtful words, crabbiness, rudeness, and hateful gestures. I don't mean to replace them with fake smiles or to put on a facade of happiness. What do non-Christians want with that? They already have that. We should live lives that bear the fruit of the Holy Spirit, lives that non-Christians would desire. The fruits of the Spirit are love, joy, peace, patience, gentleness, faith, humbleness, compassion, and kindness. These are the attributes that show the Spirit is in us and we are celebrating life. Some things do not come naturally. If this is not your life, then you need to train and discipline yourself in these fruits of the Spirit.

The morning stars sang together, and the sons of God shouted for Joy at the creation. John the Baptist leaped for joy in his mother's womb at the presence of Mary, who was carrying Jesus in her womb. There is joy in the presence of the angels over sinners' repentance. Let us rejoice and be glad and give honor to Him, for the marriage of the Lamb is come and His wife has made herself ready! (Job 38:7; Luke 1:44, 15:10; Revelation 19:7)

There is much to celebrate. There has been, there is, and there will be much celebration in heaven. Knowing this we can celebrate right now here on Earth.

I want to cry, but what good would it do?
I want to talk, but to whom?
I want to explain, but it's to their disdain.
Who will hear, that hasn't already heard?
Who will see, that hasn't already seen?
Eyes wide open in the night, but blinded in the light,
Ears that tingle with the thunder, but the whisper of wisdom they plunder.
The heart waxed with age, its hope locked in a cage.
Who will believe our report, and to whom will they resort?
They hear and ignore; they see and turn away.
I will cry, but to no avail.
I will explain, but still to your disdain.
You will hear, but not listen.
You will see, but not comprehend.
Your eyes you will refuse to open.
Your ears you will refuse to uncover.
Your heart you keep cold that it might not soften.
You will refuse to believe, and to the world you will resort.
You will turn your head and walk away in it.
You leave your scarlet prints,
As you walk through the blood at the base of the cross.

Notes

1   Doug Herman, *Faith Quake: How to survive the Aftershocks of Tragedy*, (Corsicana, Texas: Kauffman Burgess Press, Baker Book House). Used by Permission by Doug Herman.

2   Herman, 78-79

3   Oswald Chambers, *My Utmost for His Highest*, (Dodd, Mead & Company Inc. 1935/ copyright renewed 1963 Oswald Chambers Publications Association, Ltd.), November 5

4   New American Standard Bible---Updated Edition, *Life Application Study Bible*, (Copyright /2000 by Zondervan), 1632; footnote 33, 34

5   Tullian Tchividjian, *The Glorious Ruin*, (Published by David C Cook 2010), 56-57

6   Chambers, December 7

7   Chambers, December 27

8   Chambers, March 8

9   Chambers, December 11

10 Chambers, March 14

11 Chambers, February 18

12 Dr. Steven Stephens, *The Wounded Warrior*, (Multnomah Publishers, Inc./2006). *29-30*

13 Stephens, 13-15

14 Chambers, February 17

15 Chambers, December 10

16 E. Michael and Sharon Rusten, *The One Year Christian History*, (Tyndale House Publishers, Inc. /2003) 98-99

17 Rusten, *154-155*

18 Rusten, *170-171*

19 Rusten, *252-253*

20 Rusten, *388-389*

21 Rusten, *462-463*

22 Rusten, *662-663*

23 Rusten, *102-103*

24 Definition of Solitude, i.word.com/idictionary/isolitude

25 Richard J. Foster, *Celebration of Discipline; The Path to Spiritual Growth,* (HarperCollins Publishers /1978,1988,1998), 96

26 Definition of Study, Dictionary.com

27 Chambers, Oswald, December 15

28 Definition of Meditate, i.word.com/idictionary/meditate

29 Definition of Meditate, thefreedicitonary.com

30 Synonyms of Study and Meditate, thesaurus.com

31 Definition of Humble, Dicionary.com

32 Origin of Humble, oxforddictionaries. com/us/.../humble

33 Origin of Humble, etymonline.com/index.php?

34 Root Words Hum and Human, English-for-students.com/human.html

35 Hebrew word anah, biblehub.com/Hebrew/6031.htm

36 Pastor J. John, *Interview;* (Trinity Broadcasting Network/Published November 13,2014) http:/bit.ly//EuXNOB

37 Definition of Hebrew and Greek words used for worship. http://biblehub.net/searchstrongs.php?q=worship

38 Definition of Hebrew and Greek words used for fellowship. http://biblehub.net/searchstrongs.php?q=fellowship

39 Definition of Hebrew and Greek words used for confess. http://biblehub.net/searchstrongs.php?q=confess http://biblehub.com/hebrew/3034.htm

40 Greek word Anthomologeomai, http://biblehub.net/searchstrongs.php?q=acknowledge http://biblehub.com/greek/437.htm

41 Definition of Greek word exomologeo, http://biblehub.com/greek/1843.htm